We need more people like Sister Freda! This warm-hearted Kenyan nurse touches the victims of HIV/AIDS with compassion and help. She is a model for us of how one person can make a tremendous difference for people who hurt.

 KAY WARREN
Co-founder, Saddleback Valley Community Church
Lake Forest, California
and Executive Director of Saddleback Church's HIV/AIDS Initiative

Darlene and Harold Sala have invested a lifetime reaching, teaching and touching people around the world with the Good News of Jesus Christ. I have been inspired and challenged by their faithful walk, and their encouragement to leaders. Now comes this book from Darlene Sala about a Kenyan nurse who is a simple model of our Savior's love.

I think, "WOW! Sister Freda, whom I love and admire, is a blessing to Darlene, whom I love and admire... What a book!!"

What a book, indeed. Read it, enjoy it and give it to your friends. Ordinary folks can do extraordinary things when they give their lives to Christ.

 STEVE RUTENBAR
Pastor of Relief, Saddleback Valley Community Church
Lake Forest, California

D1028245

I am thrilled that God inspired Darlene Sala to document the life and ministry of Sister Freda Robinson. Serving alongside Sister Freda inspired me to rely more on the healing power of Christ in treating my patients. Her complete reliance on God, her endless energy for serving, her compassion, her skill and her limitless faith have humbled me. I pray that this story, the story of a true Spirit-filled servant of God, will encourage you to follow the teaching of Christ in Luke 10:27–37.

If you are a health care professional and have a heart for serving, please consider volunteering with Sister Freda. You won't regret it.

❧ James R. Henslick, OD, known as "Dr. Rob"
Laguna Niguel, California

Heart of Compassion, Hands of Care is a must-read for anyone who feels God's call to the mission field and especially to medical missions. Sister Freda's compassion for the poor is awe-inspiring as she emulates Jesus wherever she goes.

❧ Eithne Keegan, RN ASN
Nursing Instructor and Hospital Supervisor
International HIV/AIDS educator
Foothill Ranch, California

Inviting, informative and inspirational. *Heart of Compassion, Hands of Care* is like sitting down to tea with Freda and getting the answers to questions that invariably bubble up: Who is this remarkable woman? Where is she from? How did she begin? The essence of her life's work is captured beautifully, and each chapter draws us one step closer to understanding Sister Freda's Heart of Compassion.

🐎 ERIC M. DENTON
Pastor, Riverside, California
Founder: Siempre Para los Niños
Jackets for Jesus

Because she has compassion, commitment, total dedication and is full of the Holy Spirit, I am proud to be a prayer and financial partner with Sister Freda. Africa is a place where people are often trapped by poverty, resulting in tremendous health needs. Freda is there 24/7 taking care of orphans and the sick. It is my honor to be involved with the clinic and the nursing academy.

🐎 JOHN E. WEST
Founder and President, Keystone Mortgage Group,
Mission Viejo, California

As a doctor I have performed surgeries at Sister Freda's Cottage Hospital and have witnessed outcomes that only Our Lord Himself could pull off. It is with certainty that I can state that God is working through Sister Freda's ministry. The ground that Freda and Richard have dedicated for the Lord's work is truly "Holy Ground."

In her book *Heart of Compassion, Hands of Care* Darlene Sala presents the firsthand testimony of missionaries who have journeyed to western Kenya and experienced for themselves the love and dedication in Sister Freda that is rarely found among health care providers. This wonderful book is sure to inspire all who read it, and I endorse it wholeheartedly.

❧ DR. TIMOTHY JAMES
Podiatrist, La Jolla, California

After watching Sister Freda lovingly and patiently treat a burned child I wanted to tell her story. Darlene Sala has done it for me — and for you. It is an inspiring book that will break your heart and yet give you hope as you see God's love at work in this saintly woman.

Darlene Sala has done a wonderful job of describing a life of Christian service and love we should all aspire to. This inspiring story about an inspiring woman of God by an inspired author is a book you need to read.

I will definitely read this book to my grandchildren.

❧ DAVID HAYMES, MD
Houston, Texas

HEART of
COMPASSION
HANDS of
CARE

The story of an African woman
who refuses to ignore
disease and poverty

darlene**SALA**

WingSpread Publishers
www.wingspreadpublishers.com

WingSpread Publishers

3825 Hartzdale Drive · Camp Hill, PA 17011
www.wingspreadpublishers.com

A division of Zur Ltd.

Heart of Compassion, Hands of Care
ISBN: 978-1-60066-190-7
© 2008 by Darlene Sala

12 11 10 09 085 4 3 2 1

Cover design by Amor Aurelio B. Alvarez
Page design by Dorothy Joy Quan

Published for Wing Spread
in the Philippines
by OMF Literature Inc.
776 Boni Avenue
Mandaluyong City, Metro Manila
www.OMFLit.com

Printed in the Philippines

CONTENTS

DEDICATION

IF IT WEREN'T FOR STEVE RUTENBAR, I might never have gone
to Kenya, nor would I have met a nurse known as Sister Freda.
Nor would most of the 700-plus people he has taken there as
Pastor of Relief at Saddleback Valley Community Church in
Lake Forest, CA. Because his heart is as big as his six-foot-
seven body, Steve puts up with the whims and inexperience of
people — many of whom have never before traveled outside
the U.S., let alone to any place where poverty stares them in
the face — so that they can see and touch and, yes, even smell
need.

But after Steve shows us that
need, he doesn't leave us bur-
dened with a load of guilt for
having so much more than the
vast majority of people in this
world. Instead, he encourages us
to get involved. He challenges us
to ask God what part He wants
us to have in helping needy
people spiritually, physically, and
even economically.

To Steve, people in Kenya are not just numbers. They are people like James, who needs mentoring. And Halima, who needs a future. And Patricia, who needs specialized AIDS medicines. They include people in prison who need a hug because no one has touched them in months. They include street children in the slums who don't yet understand Jesus loves them because no one else has ever loved them.

Because Steve truly loves people, when he sees needs, he takes the hands of those who are hurting and links them with the hands of people who are able to help meet those needs. And he does it over and over and over again.

Steve, you are the bridge that has connected Sister Freda with those who can help her. You've let us see her heart and encouraged us to work with her, and to help provide for her what she does not have.

That's why this book is dedicated to you.

Darlene Sala
2008

THANK YOU

THANK YOU, THANK YOU to all who have shared with me your "Sister Freda" stories and experiences! Even if your story is not printed in the book, you have contributed greatly, for your viewpoint has broadened mine. I've glimpsed your heart; I've seen the concern in your faces; your words have conveyed the change in your lives that knowing Sister Freda has made.

Thank you, Steve, Lisa, Dean, Eithne, Tim, Mavis, David, Marilyn, Jana, John, Denise, Ezekiel, Blane, Anne, James, Tamara, Rob, Theresa, Cathy, Beth, Agnes, Dave, Elaine, Jeanne, Don, Ann, Connie, Angeline, Tara, Greg, Gloria, Denise, Terry, Sandi, George, Dorothy, Becky, Chris, Floyd, Michelle, Chuck, Sue, Daniel, Kathleen, Moses, Kelly, Dominic, Erin, Cheryl, Rich, Geoffrey, Sandy, Shem, Kathy, Kim, Rodger, Lydia and Marjaana.

Keep telling people your stories. Keep sharing your heart. Keep helping Sister Freda. Keep doing what God impresses you to do. In doing so you are touching lives for eternity.

A big thank you is due to the staff of OMF LITERATURE, along with WingSpread Publishers, for getting this book into your hands. Lindy and Karen, your careful reading in order to catch errors and inconsistencies in the manuscript, has been such a blessing, as has Joy's painstaking and precise typesetting. Thank you, one and all.

Lastly, no one who reads this book will fully know how much is owed to my daughter, Bonnie Craddick, and my husband, Harold, for making the story come alive. Although Bonnie has not yet been to Kenya or met Sister Freda, her prodding to describe vividly what I saw and experienced has greatly enriched the account: "Mom, you *know* Sister Freda. Tell us what she is like." Harold, the title idea was yours. In fact, you must have this manuscript practically memorized. Thank you, Bonnie and Harold, for sharing your literary skills and improving mine.

May the Lord be glorified!

The emotion-filled message I received from Freda Robinson, sent from Kenya following that nation's presidential election on December 27, 2007, read:

> I thank God, Darlene, that I am alive today and that my family and most of my friends and neighbors are still alive.

I felt reassured, yet still concerned for the safety of my friend, the nurse who is founder and director of Sister Freda's Medical Center,[*] a hospital, clinic, and feeding center for the poor of Kitale, in Kenya. I wondered if Freda's compassionate outreach to help Kenyans of all tribes would place her in a position of danger from those who were using violence to destroy members of any tribe that opposed theirs. I was anxious to learn from her what was happening.

Freda went on to tell that on the day of the election she rose at 5 a.m. to line up with her fellow Kenyans in order to cast votes for their councilors, members of parliament and their president. After voting, she went to work at the clinic, caring for the sick as usual.

---

[*] Officially, Sister Freda's Medical Centre. The author has chosen to use American spelling throughout the book.

She wrote:

> The next day we waited for election results all day long and into the night. On Sunday, December 29 there was tension in the air as it had taken so unusually long [to report the outcome]. The result that President Mwai Kibaki had been proclaimed the winner over Raila Odinga was revealed at around 4 p.m. Fifteen minutes later he was inaugurated for another term.
>
> Then all hell broke loose because of the live broadcast that was on television and radio where the opposition leaders of Odinga's Orange Democratic Movement (ODM) refuted the election results openly and issued statements that made the public go wild. A man who claimed to have been tallying the presidential results was fronted by the opposition leaders, saying that the winning side had stolen votes and that his conscience would not allow him to stay silent.
>
> The people started fighting and burning. [In many areas] friends and neighbors were killing one another and burning the houses of others who were supposed to be with the winning side. Husbands and wives who did not belong to the same tribe separated immediately, running in opposite directions. Wives were left alone to fend for the kids. Most of the time there was nowhere to run to for safety.
>
> Mutilated bodies of men, women and children were scattered all over. The Assemblies of God

church in Eldoret where women and children had sought refuge was burned and all perished. This was very sad. What did these innocent women and children have to do with the so-called rigged elections?

There were roadblocks between the cities, made with boulders, tree trunks, and burning tires. Drivers and passengers were asked their tribe, and if you did not belong to the "correct" tribe, you were killed instantly. Some people were hacked to death and others felled by use of a chain saw, their bodies mutilated.

People were forced to stay in their houses for days. Children and families were displaced and most went to seek refuge in churches and schools.

Then the shortage of food started biting because everyone went into panic buying. People purchased food with any money they were left with. The prices of food rocketed and there was no fuel, no public transport. The pharmacies were closed, and when they reopened, people rushed to buy out all the malaria medicine, fluids, and other essential medicines.

At night there was darkness because power transformers had been set ablaze. We had only flashlights to enable us to see at night to deliver babies and give intravenous medicines. We did not have running water as there was no fuel for the pump. It was like doom had set in.

A world that had been very peaceful last week was now flowing with blood. The neighbors that we

prayed with together in the same church, drank water with from the same river, traded with in the same
market, and exchanged greetings with, had suddenly
become enemies. Their love had turned into hate
because of politics.

The events that have taken place since I began writing the
story of Freda Robinson have changed the face of Kenya. They
have not changed its *heart* but only revealed the conflicts that
since the Mau Mau Rebellion of the 1950s have lurked just
beneath the surface of this unusually progressive African nation.

To write a book about Kenya was never my intent. This story
is about Sister Freda Robinson, a daughter of Kenya, who beyond doubt makes her nation proud. (She is called "Sister" as a
Kenyan term of respect.) Yet the incidents that followed the
Kenyan national election on December 27, 2007, so changed
the face of Africa's most democratic country that a few remarks
about Kenya are essential for understanding its people.

An outsider looking at Kenya struggles to understand. Seeing the butchery of thousands of people, the smoldering ruins
of homes, churches, businesses and farms that were built over
many years by grueling struggle and toil, and the heart-wrench-
ing displacement of some half a million Kenyans,[1] most of whom
have no home to return to, one can only ask, "Why? Why this,
in Kenya, one of Africa's most stable nations, one of her best
economies, her model of democracy?"

What caused the mayhem that followed the election? Tri-
balism? Politics? Economics? Land distribution?

I believe the answer to all of those questions is "Yes." All of these factors came together in one giant collision that caused tragic reactions wherever frustration existed. Four issues contributed to the outbreaks:

1   Inequality in land division among the forty-two or more tribes of Kenya, dating back to colonial days but exacerbated in 1963 under Kenya's first president, Jomo Kenyatta.

2   Political power in Kenya equals financial power. If you want to become rich in most countries, become a businessman. If you want to become rich in Africa, become a politician. Political position, then, becomes something to be coveted, and if obtained, to be held onto at all costs. "Most Kenyans believe they would do better economically if their tribe were in power," says journalist Edwin Okong'o.[2]

3   Inequality in economic resources among Kenyans has spawned envy and jealousy. An economy whose annual growth rate has accelerated from *minus* 1.6% in 2002 to 5.5% at time of writing has changed the plight of the poor very little.

4   During various times in Kenya, land-grabbing has resulted in bitterness, a sense of helplessness, and outright tribal war.

When people become frustrated because they cannot get justice, they feel that revenge is their only recourse against whomever they believe to be the cause. So you have Luos and

Luhyas fighting Kikuyus — not only because of racial bias or prejudice but also because of injustice.

Then fear sets in. At one point in the town of Limuru, not far from Nairobi, about 700 Luos and Luyhas were massed in the police station compound preparing to leave the area, many saying they would never return. At the other end of the town the Red Cross was caring for hundreds of Kikuyus who had migrated there the week before, from the Rift Valley in western Kenya, to escape their Kalenjin enemies.

"The reasons for [our conflicts] are that peaceful means for resolving our differences have been closed down," says Maina Kiai, chairman of the Kenya National Commission on Human Rights, "so people become violent and express that violence in an ethnic way because our politics is ethnic. That's very important to emphasize."[3]

Back before the days of colonialism "tribal structures served as the equivalents of the modern state," writes Emily Wax of the Washington Post, "and people turned to their [tribe's] leaders for loans, health care and mediation in domestic disputes."[4] In the years since 1963, when independence was granted, the Kenyan government has endeavored to meet those needs. For Kenyans, the transition from tribal governing to national governing has been anything but unproblematic. Only when the people feel they have a viable recourse to justice will trust again be established.

KENYA'S FUTURE

A popular Kiswahili saying goes, "When two elephants fight, it's the grass that suffers."[5] The actions of two men both determined to hold the office of President of Kenya have resulted in much suffering for Kenya's people. Only God knows the price that will be paid before personal agendas are subordinated to the ultimate good of the nation; however, hundreds of thousands of Kenyans on both sides of the issues are praying for a peaceful future.

Maina Kiai, one of Kenya's leading independent voices, sums it up:

> We are being confronted with the very survival of Kenya as we know it, and if we do the wrong thing, we will get into war. If we do the right thing, then maybe we'll become a much better Kenya, a much more democratic, a much more equitable society. This is a big moment for us — a constitutional moment. These things come once in a generation.[6]

"Outside Kenya we call ourselves Kenyans," writes a resident in his blog. "In Kenya we call ourselves 'Luos,' 'Kikuyus,' 'Kambas,' 'Kalenjins,' . . . the list is endless."[7]

As Mr. Kiai concludes,

> The moment is now to make a solid thing called Kenya.[8]

AFRICA

KENYA

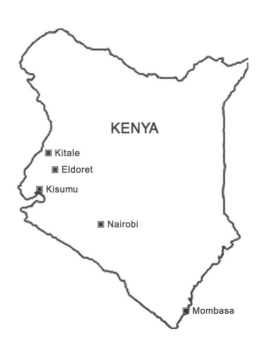

LAYOUT OF THE
MEDICAL CENTER COMPOUND

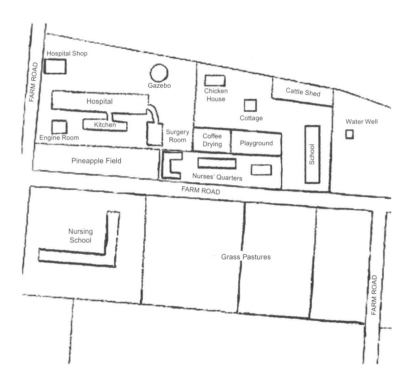

chapter 1

"THE GREAT NURSE"

The story of a life cannot be separated from the geography that forms the stage upon which the drama of that person's life is played out. Africa is an immense continent — one so large that you could place the United States, China, Europe and Alaska inside it and still have room left over. But focus with me on one African nation. . . .

The drama that unfolds in these pages takes place in Kenya — the East African nation where the massive Rift Valley has carved a gash in the vast landscape much like a sculptor might in a soft piece of clay. Flying over Kenya one gazes upon villages of small mud cottages set in circles known as *kraals*. As the plane drops down in Nairobi the view is of thousands of small shacks where people's existence is in marked contrast to life in the estates of the wealthy who live just a stone's throw away. Here, in far-flung villages and teeming cities alike, masses of people live and die, love and hate, sing and mourn, generation after generation.

The needs of the country produce a deep anguish felt in the heart by most first-time visitors. Though by no means unique to Kenya, the barefoot children in grimy, torn T-shirts that reveal their bony ribs, and their thin, fly-beleaguered faces, greet you, as does the elderly, wretched beggar with matted hair, watery eyes, and threadbare clothes covered with filth at the side of the road. "Their needs are so great and I am so powerless. How can I possibly help?" the heart cries out.

Right in the midst of it all is Freda Robinson — a nurse whose medical center cares for the poor, regardless of their inability to pay, who feeds the hungry, bandages the bleeding, rescues the orphan and envelops the AIDS patient in loving embrace. But there is something else about this 50-something-year-old quiet, resolute woman who is known to break into her delightful "happy dance" when things go well. I knew when I walked into Freda Robinson's office that she was an extraordinary lady. True, I was attracted by her open arms of welcome, her soft voice and lovely smile. I admired her silky hair with its intricate braids so artistically arranged. Yet there was something more, an intangible presence, that drew me like so many others to the one called "The Great Nurse" by her fellow Kenyans. Only moments passed before I realized it was the very presence of Jesus. Sister Freda's love of God and those He places in her path seemingly wells up from her heart and spills over. Jesus might be an intangible presence in the life of this woman, but she seeks to make Him known in very, very tangible ways.

My time with Freda on my first trip to Kenya was short. As she gave us a tour of her medical center, in the course of our conversation I asked her if her story had ever been written. She responded that no, it hadn't. I felt that tap on the shoulder that so often indicates God has a job for you to do — in this case, the task lay in a life story crying to be told. So when I returned to California, I drew up a list of thirty-five questions to help me get started. I emailed the list to Sister Freda with the comment that I realized she was too busy to answer them herself, but that maybe someone would be kind enough to write down the answers for her.

A short time later, I received an envelope from her containing nine pages of answers to my thirty-five questions, in her own handwriting. I could hardly believe that she had taken time to give me, in such detail, the information I needed.

Then I began to contact people who have worked closely with her. You'll read some of their personal experiences in the book. It impressed me that each one I spoke with seemed to feel he had gained much more from this nurse than he had given. Each one knows his life has been challenged by her vision, her humility, her courage, her compassion. And so has mine.

chapter 2

Born to Care

It was one of those clear mornings in Kitale, Kenya, where the altitude of almost 6,000 feet gave a crispness to the air. Never in his wildest imagination did the property caretaker have any idea what drama was about to unfold as he walked the dusty road to Sister Freda's Medical Clinic that morning. Ignoring the roosters that were welcoming the new day with their raucous crowing, he passed the low-slung row of concrete-block buildings with green corrugated metal roofs where patients were being treated in Sister Freda's small hospital.

He went into the shed and picked up his well-worn machete, examining the blade to make sure it would cut through the weeds and grass easily.

If this morning's routine was typical, he picked up a broad-cut file and honed the edge of his machete — a lethal weapon in the hands of an angry drunk but a tool widely used for cutting sugarcane in the fields and hacking the bush grass that quickly takes over a neglected field.

Walking to the edge of the compound where the grass was in need of attention, he went to work.

Rhythmically as he swung the blade in the dead grass, the machete sang with a *whish, whish, whish.* Then he heard something out of place. It was faint but it was definitely extraordinary. Laying down the machete, he dropped to his knees and parted the bush grass.

Absolutely unbelievable! But there he was — a tiny baby boy. He looked to be about a week old, the umbilical cord still attached.

At first the caretaker wasn't even sure that the baby was alive. Indeed, he had been just inches from death, the man's blade had come so close to his tiny body. It was a miracle he was found, and uninjured. Sobering too to realize that if he had not been discovered as he was, he would have drowned, for a very heavy rain and hail were to fall later that day, which would have inundated the newborn child. Or he would certainly have died from exposure and hunger.

The tiny boy was brought to Sister Freda, who could not help but wonder, "How did this child get here?" Had the mother been trying to get to the hospital and had the baby on the way? Did a distraught mother give birth to the baby in the village nearby and then — like Jochebed, the mother of Moses who put her infant son in a basket made of papyrus — did she place the baby in the grass, quite certain that someone from the hospital would find him?

Of course, what else could she name the child? "His name will be Moses," Sister Freda quietly announced. Like baby Moses in the Old Testament, he was found in time and saved from death. Today, under Freda's care, he is a beautiful, healthy child.

Who is this Sister Freda — nurturer of abandoned children, shivering malaria patients, bloody victims of tribal skirmishes, widows left with nothing but AIDS, savior of those unable to save themselves?

Here is the story of a woman's life, a woman herself born in poverty with neither resources nor family connections, but with a simple faith — a fearless, unrelenting faith in a sovereign God. It is the story of a woman who lacked much but depended much upon the supply of a God who says, "My grace is sufficient for you, for my power is made perfect in weakness," 2 Corinthians 12:9.

When she was born her parents named her Freda Nyanga Mukhweso.

The African sun was just cresting the mountains behind the little village of Malava in central western Kenya, a conglomeration of small, one-room houses made of sun-dried red mud pressed onto frames of sticks and plastered with cow dung.

"Wake up, Freda — wake up!"

Freda tried to ignore her mother's voice as she pulled the thin cover closer around herself, wishing for just a few more minutes of sleep. But then Freda felt Mama Eldah's firm but gentle hand on her shoulder. "It is time to get the water so I can fix your father's tea. Come now, the empty pot is just outside the door."

Every morning at daybreak, Freda's first chore of the day was to put the heavy clay pot on her head and go to the river to bring back the family's water supply. It was a 40-minute walk over rough, dusty ground, with small stones making themselves felt under her bare feet. Then it was another 40 minutes retracing her steps back home as she carried the old stained pot on her head, now so much heavier with its more than five gallons of water. As she reached her house, she bent to enter the low doorway, carefully easing the pot to the ground. Woe to the child who broke the family water pot! A disaster equivalent in America to crashing the family car!

Who would ever have dreamed that this little girl, born and raised in a remote tribal area of Kenya, would one day be used by God to bring the Water of Life — both physical and spiritual life — to hundreds, perhaps thousands, of people? People thirsty for someone to care. People who need to see God through the heart and hands of someone who reaches out to them in compassion.

THE EARLY YEARS

Fetching water was not Freda's only job by any means — not even her primary job. As a very young girl she milked the cows and then hawked the milk at the marketplace. To carry it there in its big jar, she had a choice of two routes: either an hour-long walk around the forest, or the shorter half-hour route that cut directly through the forest but where she risked attack by a stalking hyena, a poisonous snake, a lion or a fearsome Cape buffalo. Not surprisingly, Freda became the fastest runner in her school — because of her "cross-country training" taking the milk to market through the forest.

There was schoolwork, of course, and the ever-present work on the farm and the household chores. But Freda's most important responsibility was taking her turn tending the cattle, the family's most critical asset. Before Freda's father married her mother, he had owned twelve cows. But he had given all but one of them to meet the bride price demanded by his future father-in-law. Because he had to rebuild a herd from scratch, every cow was now doubly precious to the family.

Freda grew up in a region bordering the Rift Valley, an area of hills and valleys, mountains and small indigenous forests, and everywhere — rocks. She learned to be adept at crossing rivers on fallen trees because there were no bridges. Growing up in this rural environment, she was well acquainted with the wild animals of the area — leopards, baboons, hyenas, monkeys, various birds and the exquisite butterflies she loved to chase.

Everyone in her family worked hard — Mama, Daddy, her two brothers and her sister. Born in 1950, Freda was the youngest of the four children. Though the family never had much money, somehow they had enough to eat. Like most of the people in their area, Freda's parents were, for the most part, struggling subsistence farmers, growing only enough maize[1] and sugarcane to survive.

Mama Eldah was a staunch Christian who instilled in her children the fear of God and biblical values, values shaping Freda into the person she is today. They attended Malava Friends (Quaker) Church. In fact, one of Freda's earliest memories is of going there with her sister to Sunday school. But beyond church attendance, Mama stressed the significant value of knowing

God and having a personal relationship with Him. Together they prayed earnestly for Daddy Mariko, who at that time was heavily into the world's pleasures. Freda was ten years old when their prayers were finally answered.

What happened did not seem at first to be an answer to prayer, for one evening Daddy Mariko simply did not come home. All that night Mama Eldah listened for his footsteps, but he did not return. Fear began to grip her heart. Where could he be? He had said nothing about leaving.

Actually, when Daddy Mariko left Malava, he himself didn't know where he was headed. Getting on a bus and traveling to the end of one line, he then rode one bus after another until at last he found himself in Mombasa on the Kenyan coast, 750 miles from Malava. There, rambling through the streets, despondent and without hope, he stumbled into a church. Falling on his knees in desperation, he asked God to forgive him of his past and to take over his life. When Daddy Mariko rose to his feet, he was a new man. With newfound joy he made his way back home to his family.

Seeing her daddy walk through the doorway, Freda ran to him. Eager to show him her latest injury, her big toe that had had the nail torn off, she knew, when immediately he gathered her in his arms and began to comfort her, that he was radically changed. While for some people spiritual growth may be very gradual, for Daddy Mariko it was exponential. From that time on, he immersed himself in reading, obeying and teaching the Scriptures. Their family life was utterly transformed.

Freda received her basic education at the village primary school in Malava. Here her young heart was stirred by the sight of villagers, especially children, who were sick and needy, thin and lethargic, with a look of hopelessness in their eyes. Moved with compassion, Freda shared with them food, clothing, and whatever she had. She asked her parents to help as well. This early habit of sharing was a precursor to her life work ahead, caring for the poor.

The lives of many villagers were transformed by young Freda's empathetic intervention. One day there was a knock on the door. A middle-aged woman had come to their home seeking work on their farm. She looked so frail, weak and sickly that little Freda was immediately concerned. The woman, she discovered, had given birth to a child only three days before, but already she was forced to find work in order to provide for her family.

"Oh, Mama, let's help her. But don't make her work on the farm," Freda pled. "Let's give her some food and money so she can start a business." Already Freda was learning the skills of gentle persuasion that she would need in sticky situations ahead.

Although Mama Eldah loved to have visitors in their home, she knew she would have to contend with Freda's generous spirit. Once as they were sipping the sweet Kenyan tea her mother had served in traditional wooden cups, Freda asked their guest, "Do you have cups at your house?"

"No, we don't." was the reply.

"Well, we have three. Mama, can't we give them one of ours?"

At one time when Freda was a child, her mother became very ill. Freda had noticed that people picked leaves and tree bark, steeping them into a drink that helped sick people get well. So Freda proceeded to make a "brew" for her mother and bring it to her to drink. Mama Eldah wisely invented an excuse to get Freda to leave the room so she could pour out the drink, knowing it might well be poisonous. Only years later did Freda learn what had happened to her "tea." In her growing-up years, Freda did, however, gain experience in the practice of herbal medicine that has healed for centuries when manufactured medicine is not available. For instance, Freda learned that if a mother giving birth is bleeding profusely, chewing on common ordinary pumpkin root will stop the bleeding — life-saving knowledge in a rural area!

Freda's life was basically simple. The one new dress she received each year was precious because she knew her mother had walked 20 miles to town to buy this "for church only" dress. On Monday through Friday she wore her school uniform, and on Saturdays she wore either her old dress or last year's uniform, a pattern still followed by most Kenyan children today.

One of Freda's despised chores was to smear fresh cow dung on the floor of their home every week, to cover the dirt so that fleas would not be a problem. Even though the practice is commonplace in Kenyan culture, Freda hated the task and would put it off as long as possible. On one occasion her mother assigned her this chore and then left the house. Freda delayed getting started, until suddenly she realized that she couldn't get the whole job done before her mother was to return. Quickly she smeared just the entrance and doorway with the smelly muck — and none too soon.

"What a good job you did, Freda," complimented her mother — until she stepped through the doorway. "Oh, my goodness," she exclaimed. But by then Freda was wisely nowhere to be found.

When Mama Eldah became seriously ill with malaria and typhoid fever, Freda had to drop out of school for a month to care for her — another foreshadowing of her life's calling. Every family member's work was necessary for survival, so in addition to nursing her mom, Freda took over her mother's chores — finding firewood, cooking, washing, and cultivating vegetables and pineapple.

Mama Eldah recovered, and a short time later the family moved from Malava to Kitale, a distance of about 75 miles. It was a time of tremendous change for young Freda. The contrasts between Malava and Kitale were immense. Malava is a rural town in the North Rift region of Kenya. Kitale is a city on the east-west trade route that serves as the seat of government for the Trans-Nzoia Administrative District of Rift Valley Province. Kitale has quite a history, for the city was once a relay station on the slave route between Uganda and Tanzania. Slaves were quartered at what is now the Kitale Golf Club.

In addition, Freda was now old enough for secondary school (the equivalent of high school in the U.S.). But she did not go to school in Kitale. Instead she attended Nasokol Girls' Secondary School, a boarding school which was 20 miles from Kitale — her first time away from home. She had all the jitters of any girl's first day at a new school. "Will I fit in? Will I make friends? I already miss my mom!"

TEEN YEARS

Because she had enrolled late, Freda was at her new school only one month when the term ended. Returning home for the school break, excited about her new experience, she was unprepared for the bombshell that was to fall. She learned she would have to withdraw from secondary school in order to marry a man she did not know, the husband her parents had chosen for her. The man was a university graduate and held two degrees. Her parents reasoned that he seemed mature and the type of man who would take good care of their daughter. So at age fifteen she was pressured into an arranged marriage.

No matter how Freda resisted, her efforts were in vain because her parents had already been paid the dowry for her marriage. Girls in Kenya are an economic commodity; sometimes among the impoverished, marrying off a daughter is the only remaining way to provide some small income for the family. Frequently a daughter has been forced to marry in order to provide for her brothers' education.[2]

All Freda's dreams lay in tatters as she began married life in a relationship doomed from the beginning. Even long into her marriage, Freda knew very little about the man she had married. Incredibly, she was pregnant with her fourth child before she knew her husband's true vocation, discovering he was a lawyer and not a teacher.

Freda became a servant in her own home, living with many relatives who really ruled the place. Determined not to be held down by ignorance in a marriage that was bitterly difficult, Freda enrolled for her Ordinary Level Examination (the equivalent of a high school diploma in the U.S.). Friends sneaked schoolbooks to her so she could study, and she passed all her subjects with 'B's even though it was hard to prepare adequately. On one occasion, she did not have time to read the whole history book, so she let the book fall open, read the section that was in front of her, and took the test. How grateful she was that the exam focused on the section she had read! Remarkably, she took her final exam three days after giving birth to her fourth child, achieving the second highest result in her school.

Life with her husband eventually proved to be untenable. In spite of humiliation and suffering, God was faithful to her, enabling her to pass her examinations, which paved the way for her training in nursing. The marriage was dissolved.

FREDA BECOMES A NURSE

In 1974, when her youngest child, Stella, was two years old, Freda enrolled in the Nairobi School of Nursing, graduating as a registered nurse in 1978. From then on she became known as "Sister" Freda, the Kenyan term of respect for all nurses. During her training, her older three children, Emma, Michael, and Erick, stayed with her parents. At the time, Freda's sister was living and working in Nairobi and helped her financially, as did her parents. Stella had her first day of school while they were living in Nairobi and, in fact, when Sister Freda returned to Kitale, Stella remained to receive her education in the capital city.

WORK AT MT. ELGON HOSPITAL

In 1979, Sister Freda was employed for three months as a nurse assisting in outpatient surgery at Mt. Elgon Hospital in Kitale. Later that same year she trained for one year in midwifery at Mater Misercodiae Hospital in Nairobi. When she returned to Mt. Elgon Hospital, she was promoted to Hospital Matron, which means she served as hospital administrator, in charge of all departments, including Pharmacy and Doctors' Assistance. Her keen mind enabled her to reel off the technical names of the medicines — and spell them correctly — as easily as she was able to recall people's names.

The experience gained in this very responsible position was invaluable to Freda when she later opened her own medical center, for she was already able to do "everything" in the hospital except the actual work of a physician — though now she will even perform surgery in emergency situations.

While working at Mt. Elgon Hospital, Sister Freda had an experience she will never forget. She had finished her work for the day and returned home. But no sooner had she entered the doorway of her house than she felt an unmistakable urging to return to the hospital. Try as she might, she could not brush it aside. Immediately she turned around and went back to the hospital.

As Sister Freda re-entered the hospital compound, the lovely bougainvillea and hibiscus and flowering vines that she usually admired did not catch her attention, so strong was the impulse in her heart. Quickly she strode through the door and down the hallway. Passing by the prenatal care ward, she peeked in at the babies, for children have always had a soft spot in Sister Freda's heart. Then suddenly she stopped. One baby caught her well-trained eye and set off a red alert in her heart. This little boy didn't appear to be breathing. Rushing to the incubator, she snatched him up and began to massage his heart and give him mouth-to-mouth resuscitation.

"I felt the guiding hand of God that day," recalls Sister Freda. "As I worked with him, he gasped once. I gave him oxygen and he began to breathe normally — and today Mr. Korir is an attorney in Kitale."

About this time, Sister Freda acquired her first car. And not just *any* car, but a late model Audi. This was the outcome of doing private nursing for the wife of a gentleman who held a rather high position in government. Eventually his wife died, and in appreciation for Sister Freda's skilled nursing care, the man gave to Sister Freda his wife's fine car.

But the vehicle almost became her coffin. It happened when a wild driver forced her off the paved highway. She managed to maneuver the car back onto the road but could not fully regain control. No vehicles were coming from the opposite direction at the time, something of a miracle in Kenya.

"Oh, God, help me," Sister Freda cried in desperation. Suddenly the car, as if under the control of another, went into a 180° skid, stopping abruptly.

Seeing what happened, three men in a pick-up truck pulled up next to her car. "Congratulations!" they exclaimed, reaching though the window to shake hands with Sister Freda.

"Why? Why are you congratulating me?" she asked, still trembling.

"For the way you controlled your car."

Sister Freda knew that only God had been in control! She appeared to be so shaken that the men suggested, "Why don't you just sit here for a few minutes and then decide which direction you want to go."

"Does my car still have tires?" Sister Freda asked, convinced the tires must have blown out.

"Yes, they're all fine." But after the men left, Sister Freda got out and walked around her car to just to be sure. No one needed to convince her that God had spared her life and had work for her to do in the future.

Mt. Elgon Hospital, where Sister Freda worked, is a private institution built by Europeans and run by trustees. Everyone pays for his own care, and demands for quality nursing are high. In stark contrast however, the immediate neighboring hospital is the district government hospital, which, of course, is cheaper. Its doors are open for everybody, especially the poor. The government hospital processes 1000 inpatients a day, plus those treated in the outpatient clinic. Overcrowding is inevitable, and, when necessary, beds are shared. The quality of care is far from optimum. But only those with a comfortable income can afford to be treated at Mt. Elgon.

Sister Freda served the patients of Mt. Elgon Hospital until 1988, when, thanks to the kindness of one of her patients, her dream of studying abroad came true. A British woman whom she had treated at Mt. Elgon Hospital learned of Freda's desire to pursue additional training in Canada, and provided a scholarship for her. Once again her sister and parents cared for Freda's children, this time so that she could complete a six-month medical program at the University of Alberta in Edmonton. There Freda was able to study Hospital Administration, Trends and Issues in Nursing, Tropical Diseases, and Surgical Theatre, all of which were to be invaluable to her future ministry.

Completing her study in Canada, Sister Freda returned to Mt. Elgon Hospital, serving on staff until 1995. But day by day as she worked, she began to sense a stirring in her heart. God was increasingly burdening her heart for the village people in the slum areas surrounding Kitale, who had so little medical help available to them. Sister Freda could not get them out of her mind.

As she drove to work, she saw those who were seriously ill crawling for miles on their hands and knees from the outskirts of the city to get to the district hospital for treatment. "Sometimes the effort of dragging themselves to the hospital was too much; some of those trying to reach the hospital didn't make it. It was heartbreaking to see their dead bodies lying along the road." Speaking of the suffering that most touches her heart, her voice drops with intense emotion.

"All of Kitale saw them too but few felt any personal responsibility to get involved. Sadly, the wealthy people did little or nothing to help," Sister Freda adds with evident irritation, her words coming rapidly.

"This is wrong, wrong, wrong! They live so far from the hospital, and there is no way for them to get there without terrible hardship. They're so poor they can't afford even a *boda-boda* [bicycle taxi] ride. There should be medical care near where these people live so they can get help. I felt a compulsion to get involved."

Thus was planted in her heart the seed that would grow into a medical clinic and eventually a hospital for the poor. Like the Good Samaritan, Sister Freda could not leave these people lying by the side of the road with no hope of help. Determined to alleviate their painful existence and answer the cry of her own heart, she agonized over how she could help. She had no money, no connections — only a burden to help, and God-given compassion.

"Lord, what do I do?"

ENTER RICHARD

He was a handsome Englishman born in Zambia who moved to Kenya in 1953. His parents, both English by birth, met and married in Zambia, where his father was a metallurgist in the copper mines. Sister Freda and Richard Robinson became acquainted in 1980 when visiting a mutual friend in Kitale. A short time later, Sister Freda began caring for Richard's wife, whom she loved very much. But in 1995, after a long illness, Mrs. Robinson passed away.

Richard was a prominent citizen in Kitale, owning at one time 2000 acres of land with fine trees and the best cows in the area. He was looked up to as a leader in this city of nearly 200,000 people. Seeing through Freda's eyes, Richard, too, became concerned for the almost insurmountable needs that he saw. He caught her vision. Following the death of his wife, their relationship grew.

In 1996, Sister Freda began holding mobile clinics on a piece of land Richard owned in the village of Birunda, ten miles outside of Kitale Town. This acreage was adjacent to the very villages where the poor had settled when tribal conflicts in their home provinces had forced them to move. It was an ideal location for a medical facility where needy people could come for help.

By faith Freda and Richard started construction of a two-room clinic later that year, adding a surgical facility in 1997. Then, in 1998, although they did not have sufficient funds to achieve their dream of turning the clinic into a hospital, they were inspired to press on by 2 Corinthians 5:7, which says "We live by faith, not by sight," and by Psalm 121, which says, "My help comes from the Lord, the Maker of heaven and earth."

A MEDICAL CENTER IS BORN

Urged on by the appalling needs that existed, Sister Freda felt compelled to take early retirement in her 40s from her prestigious position at Mt. Elgon Hospital, in order to work full-time establishing the medical center. Richard sold all his land and supported her in the medical work. From the beginning they made the joint decision that set apart their facility from the others in the city: they would offer care to people regardless of their ability to pay.

But medical work was not the only thing on Richard's mind during these busy years. Freda's soft laugh and loving heart had won his, and Richard was determined to have more than a working relationship with Freda. Finally, in 2001, Richard's romantic pursuit of Sister Freda succeeded. The word Freda uses to describe Richard's determination to win her heart is "persistent!" Time and time again over a six-year period he came to her home to urge her to marry him, and, at last, following dinner one evening, Freda said, "Yes."

Freda and Richard Robinson were married in a colorful ceremony held in the Kabaras area, where Freda's home village was located. In Richard, Sister Freda has found a further source of strength with which to carry out her calling both in nursing and in helping the needs of the community. Watching them work together, one can see so clearly that each completes the other.

Richard and Freda form a non-typical African family. First, theirs is a mixed-race marriage. But together they have bridged the gap between African and Western cultures. California Pastor Chuck Wells, who has spent many hours with Richard and Sister Freda, commented to me, "You sense a different flavor talking to the two of them. Sister Freda's language skills, education, medical skills and range of experience are far broader and more extensive than the average African's. Yet she understands poverty. Richard has a business background and British heritage. His provision of the land that is now the compound is a vital part of the total picture. There is a distinctiveness about the two of them."

The present medical center stands on twenty-eight acres of land incorporating a small farm that provides their main income. Because of Richard's "green thumb," the farm thrives, providing maize, pineapple, mangos, guavas, tomatoes, avocados, bananas, papayas and a variety of vegetables. The animals — cows, pigs, sheep, geese, and chickens — provide food, or are sold to supply additional income. The farm also gives Sister Freda a place to grow the plants she needs for the natural remedies which she is so skilled in making — her "outdoor pharmacy."

The hospital runs in the negative financially because Sister Freda does not turn people away just because they cannot pay. Out of a hundred patients, perhaps only two can pay, and Freda simply writes off their bills. With the farm, the center manages to break even, but there is never enough for emergencies, breakdowns, needed equipment, sufficient medical supplies, or the clinics Sister Freda conducts in outlying areas. Far less could this income provide for any physical expansion of the facility.

Without outside financial contributions, the work would not have been able to continue. Those who have come to visit Freda's work have caught her vision and have donated funds to enlarge the facility so that what began as a mobile clinic has become "Sister Freda's Medical Center": a 30-bed hospital with two rooms for surgeries, an outpatient facility, medical wards, maternity care, a pediatric ward, X-ray facilities, a laboratory, pharmacy, a dental clinic, and a vision department, as well as a pre-school and feeding program.

chapter 3

LIFE-SAVING HOSPITAL CARE

Although Sister Freda is a nurse, not a doctor, when there is a life to be saved and no doctor is available, she will do everything in her power, including Caesarean sections and even amputations. When asked how she could do surgery, she says, "I put the scalpel in my hand and ask God to guide me."

One man was brought to the hospital because his feet and legs had been badly burned in a fire. His diabetes led to neuropathy, leaving him without feeling in his feet. For this reason he didn't realize they were being burned. Because there was no doctor available and the treatment was urgent, Sister Freda's carefully manicured hands moved deftly to amputate three toes and one of the suffering man's legs. The man recovered, exceedingly grateful for what she had done for him.

Pastor Steve Rutenbar, who brings missions teams every year to Kenya, was staying in a cottage at the Kitale Club, the hotel where the current team was housed, when in the middle of the night he heard someone tapping on his window. He was most surprised to find Violet, a hotel staff member who was in labor and soon to deliver her baby. How relieved Steve was that he could take her to Sister Freda's hospital, for there Violet's breach-position baby was safely delivered by C-section — and named Steven.

People get to the hospital by a variety of ways: on foot, by *matatu* (a sort of van-taxi), by *boda-boda* (bicycle taxi), and some are carried there on make-shift stretchers, mattresses or blankets. Volunteer Jana O'Guin came to the hospital one day and learned that a woman had been carried in the night before on someone's shoulder. She was extremely ill and had been brought in to die. Blood tests showed that she had AIDS. Yet Sister Freda did not give up on her but treated her with IVs and available meds — and in time she was able to walk out of the hospital on her own.

One day a little boy who couldn't speak just "showed up" at the hospital. Though he was five years old, he was so undernourished that he looked to be only two. Sister Freda permitted him to live at the hospital because he had nowhere to go, and fed him until he became healthy. Later, she and Richard personally funded his acceptance at a home for disabled children in Eldoret, seeing that the home could better help him.

On one of Pastor Steve's earliest visits to Sister Freda, he arrived at the compound laden with plastic tubs full of various medicines worth thousands of dollars.

"Hello, Freda!" he called to her, as he approached.

Now, understand that Pastor Steve was greeting a woman who moves with grace and poise — a lady of composure and dignity who under her white smock always wears skirts. Ordinarily ready with a hug for women and a welcoming curtsey for men, Sister Freda on this occasion did not greet him at all, but instead, bolted like a streak of lightning right past him down the road as fast as she could go.

Steve was taken aback by this out-of-character behavior of Sister Freda, usually the personification of warmth and courtesy in a land where no business is conducted without first observing the proper greetings. In disbelief at what he was seeing, he watched as she chased after a man riding away on a boda-boda. Sister Freda was running — and yelling! At last she caught the man's attention, and the boda-boda driver brought his rider back to the compound. Only then did Steve learn that minutes before he arrived, she had had to turn this seriously-ill man away from the hospital because she had no medicines with which to treat him. Steve had brought the medicines at precisely the right moment, with exactly what was needed to treat the man's illness. In Sister Freda's list of priorities, when a man's life is in the balance, greetings can wait — even in Kenya!

The joy that Sister Freda's Medical Center brings to people was expressed by one Kenyan woman who gave birth there: "All I can say is that it is just the right place for a mother to have her baby — so clean — and the staff is so friendly! It is a gorgeous place to be."

From the start, Sister Freda's driving force was the great need for a superior facility for the poor that would be near their slum villages, so that desperately ill people would not have to commute for medical care. During outbreaks of disease, such as the malaria season, word is sent throughout the neighborhood for locals to come to the hospital for life-saving treatment.

Knowing that help is available, many come from other parts of the city as well, traveling long distances, sometimes walking on foot for many miles. Occasionally, some have even been airlifted from other areas of Kenya in order to be treated.

In light of the reality that only a few patients can afford to cover even part of the cost of their treatment, Sister Freda's policy contrasts starkly with the policies of the public hospitals, where they insist that payment be made "up front" before treatment is given. Can you imagine a person with a raging fever or perhaps a severed artery, who comes to a hospital only to be turned away because he has no money to pay? Sister Freda is adamant that this should never happen at her Medical Center! That is why hundreds — even thousands — consider her their angel of hope.

WORKING WITH SISTER FREDA
by Eithne

I encountered Sister Freda on my first visit to Africa, as I stepped down from the Akamba bus after an eight-hour trip through the Rift Valley. She and I are both nurses, and from our first meeting I could see that my life was about to change. Little did I know, however, that she would launch me into a global campaign for HIV/AIDS. She would encourage me to "walk the walk" instead of just "talking the talk" in my Christian life.

After showing me the 30-bed facility that she operates, she took me to another hospital in Kitale district, and I saw that it could not measure up to the wonderful, peaceful environment she has at her little hospital out in the country.

On this visit to the hospital my eyes were first opened to the terrible plight of those with HIV/AIDS. We visited the HIV/AIDS ward, where there were four patients in one bed.

I saw a young boy lying on a bed with nothing on, nothing covering him. It was impossible to get him out of my mind.

"Surely something can be done," I thought. "Something *has* to be done!" I am a nursing instructor as well as a hospital supervisor, but nothing had prepared me for this terrible trauma. Sister Freda stood by my side and held my hand. Then she took me back to her hospital and I saw what a blessing she was to her people and what a difference there was between the two hospitals.

For three weeks I worked with Sister Freda. I visited the jungle home of a man who had recently died of AIDS. Actually, I visited the *two* homes where he had lived, as they stood side by side. Dirty water ran in rivulets between the houses. Nearby was a huge ditch with stagnant water that was alive with mosquitoes. In one house lived his wife and nine kids (she had just given birth to the ninth). In the other lived his mistress and her eight kids. She was pregnant with her ninth child, and all of them had AIDS. Both women were in their 30s. The question that automatically rises [in the mind of a Westerner] is: Why would this man have eighteen children in circumstances like this? The answer? So they would all have someone to take care of them in their declining years, if any survived.

Back at the hospital I watched Sister Freda reach out to one person after another. A nurse came to her for medical care because she had malaria. The woman's husband had been taking quinine for his malaria and lost his hearing, a side effect of the medication. Sister Freda gave her a job at the hospital and offered to deliver the baby she was expecting without charge. I was able to help deliver that nurse's baby, a girl, and listened to Sister Freda praying throughout the baby's delivery. Later I asked her about her prayers.

"Did you think the baby or mother was dying?"

Sister Freda answered me so kindly. "Sister Eithne, we must put our total faith in God. When we do not have the conveniences of the Western world, we rely solely on God to take care of our needs. We pray because God answers our prayers."

Can you believe that the mother gave the baby my name, Eithne — a pure Irish name? In addition, Sister Freda paid for the woman's husband to go to Nairobi to see if anything could be done about his hearing loss, but, sadly, the only help would be a cochlear implant — at a cost of $25,000.

"Sister Eithne, we need Fansidar to treat malaria, and we don't have it, and the pharmacy in town is completely out of it," said Sister Freda to me one day, "so we need to pray." I was amazed that almost immediately the pharmacy received a shipment and delivered it to the hospital.

Sister Freda conducts medical clinics wherever needed. While I was there she conducted one in Kipsongo, probably the worst slum area of Kitale. I am a very strong person, but what I saw brought me to my knees. Tears rolled down my cheeks as we ministered in prayer to these people. People there construct makeshift houses out of plastic bags.

Glue-sniffing is rampant in the slum of Kipsongo; it's a habit which kills children's brain cells but helps them forget the hunger pangs, the lonely life, their poverty and the fact that they are abandoned by their families. I remembered Matthew 19:14, where Jesus said, "Let the little children come to me, do not hinder them, for the kingdom of heaven belongs to such as these." Sister Freda follows these godly principles as she feeds these "glue boys," and God's grace and mercy shine from her like a beacon of light in the dark world of Kipsongo.

Sister Freda also conducts feeding programs in the slum areas surrounding the hospital, giving them beans, rice, flour and *ugali*.[1] I watched her treating the Turkana tribal people and the people in the Kakuma refugee camp on the border of Kenya and Uganda, home to 100,000 displaced persons. She deworms the tribal children in the Mt. Elgon area. She has compassion on those who cannot help themselves, such as the man with dementia who comes every month to the hospital, knowing Sister Freda will put money in his hand.

Sister Freda said to me one day, "Sister Eithne, all you have to do is to be present — and pray. You don't have to *do* anything — just be there and pray." I too am convinced we need to practice the power of presence. We need to reach out in love and hug these people as they are so hungry for touch.

I will never forget her words to me: "Eithne, God will take care of you if you follow Him."

Sister Freda taught me in her humble way to walk in the shoes of the poor and the left-behind of society. I strive daily to mentor others as she has mentored me. She is the role model that has led me to be so passionately involved in global missionary nursing, primarily in the area of education and training of people infected and affected by HIV/AIDS.

chapter 4

THE POWER OF PRAYER

> You can do more than pray after you have
> prayed, but you cannot do more than pray until
> you have prayed.
>
> John Bunyan[1]

To do what she does, Sister Freda is dependent on God to bring healing and to touch the hearts of those who can contribute to meet the financial needs. When she has no medicines to treat the people, you will hear her softly entreating God in fervent, earnest prayer as she goes about her work. More than once, in answer to her prayer, someone has arrived at the hospital with a donation of medicine that is exactly what she needed at the time. In fact, prayer is a dynamic part of all of Sister Freda's ministry. When Marilyn Mohr was working there as hospital administrator, first thing each morning Sister Freda would grab her and say, "We've got to go to the hospital and pray."

"We would go from bed to bed and pray for each patient," said Marilyn, "not just once but *every* morning." Every patient is prayed for every day, because Sister Freda knows that God is ultimately the one who heals. Sister Freda has a saying, "We give the medicine and pray; God heals."

"At times when we've had no medicine," she says, "we've prayed for God's hand to heal, and people have been healed — even from malaria and other diseases." Sister Freda and her staff work very, very hard. But when they can do no more, God steps in and does the impossible. Whereas physicians in the West depend on medicine to cure everything, and God is secondary, Sister Freda depends on God to cure everything, and also gives medicine.

"When I have no meds to treat wounds, I've simply used soap and water, and wounds have healed. We have two small operating theaters and have never had sepsis [which is more than many U.S. hospitals can say!] After an operation, such as Caesarean section, patients are discharged in three days and come back for stitch removal on the seventh day. Often they go home on foot or bicycle. That's when we know God has stepped in and done the rest of the healing."

Lisa Romesburg, who organizes the groups that Pastor Steve brings to Kenya, tells me that in front of Sister Freda's bedroom window are some hassocks, or ottomans. Every morning Sister Freda spends the first two hours of her day kneeling there with her prayer list that simply doesn't end. Two hours! This is her priority — and not because she doesn't have anything else to do! Of course, this personal prayer time is then followed by prayer with each patient. Truly, Sister Freda runs on prayer. No wonder when I first met her, I felt the presence of Jesus so strongly. In writing this book I have interviewed many people who know and have worked with Sister Freda, and one person after another told me they too immediately sensed God's Spirit in her life in an unusual way.

From time to time, people who visit Sister Freda write on the Internet of their encounters. Not all of the blogs are posted by believers. But even before I read what they have written, I think to myself, "I'm fairly certain that at the end of this story, I'm going to read that Sister Freda had prayer with them before they left her compound." I have been right every time.

Shirley Zimmer tells about a similar experience on a ministry trip with Sister Freda:

> After the long drive out to West Pokot, when others were resting, Sister Freda asked me if I wanted to go with her to the river to see if she could assist some of the locals. I went, and my two teens tagged along. Sister Freda spoke with a few of the women but there weren't many out that afternoon. Then she turned to Bradley, who is 14, took his hand and asked him to take a walk down the river with her. When she returned she invited Megan, 18, to take a walk. Later, when I questioned them what they talked about, they said she wanted to pray for them. She prayed for their safety, health, obedience to God, and for His guidance in their future.

I asked Sister Freda how she had learned to pray.

"I learned from my childhood that God answers prayer," she told me. "My grandparents were Christians, and in the Friends Church that we attended, prayer was stressed. We sang songs about prayer, and Ruth, my Sunday school teacher, taught us a lot about prayer.

"But I really learned about prayer for myself when as a child I was taking the milk to market. Before I took the shortcut through the forest, I would stop and earnestly pray that God would keep me safe from the wild animals, for the danger was very real. And He did just that."

THE DIFFERENCE IS THE GOD PART
by Kathy

On my first trip to Kitale, our group visited another hospital that is operated primarily to treat the poor. The team brought the hospital large amounts of medications, some of which are unobtainable in Kitale. How needed they were! In the entire hospital there was one bottle of malaria medicine, and it had been poured into a Jack Daniels whiskey bottle. The dentist there was extracting teeth without anesthesia.

I am a nurse, and I was deeply moved by what I saw. A man with extensive burns stood in front of an unscreened, open window. One child screamed as she saw us; her mother explained that the child thought we were ghosts because she had never seen a white person before! Our hearts went out to the people who were crowded two, and even three to a bed. No sheets or blankets were supplied, as the families were responsible for this.

As we walked through the hospital, we noticed a boy who looked to be about ten years old, lying unconscious by a wall in the back, directly on the concrete in the broiling sun. He was wearing a blue sweater but was naked from the waist down. Fluid was draining from his head, and he was incontinent.

At first we thought this was the morgue and the child was dead. As several of us approached him we were shocked that he stirred. Our shock turned to disbelief that this human being, a child, was sick and left alone on the ground in the hot afternoon sun. We were going to pick him up and give him water, but the staff stopped us. They did not want us to touch him. Angry with the staff and ignoring their instructions, some of the team helped him up, gave him water to drink, and asked the staff to return him to his bed. With hydration he regained some strength. We learned that the boy had been living at the hospital for some time and was a burden. When he had become ill his family, unable to care for him, had simply dumped him there, and it appeared that it would have been easier for the hospital if the boy had just died.

The next ministry team that went to Kitale reported that, surprisingly, the boy did recover and was still living at the hospital.

This hospital was such a sharp contrast to Sister Freda's Medical Center. The missing piece is the God part — love, compassion, and prayer. The doctors, nurses and administrators at the other hospital are short-handed and some of them seem impersonal and uncaring. Sister Freda's love for her patients makes the atmosphere at her hospital obviously different — a warm environment for healing.

Sister Freda is *there* for people, beyond just providing surgery and medications.

chapter 5

PROMPTED BY COMPASSION

HELP FOR WIDOWS

In addition to medical care, Sister Freda deals out great helpings of encouragement and prayer, especially for widows. She helps them move from makeshift, substandard housing structures to much-improved, semi-permanent homes and enables them to earn small incomes from selling vegetables and fruit.

One morning while Marilyn Mohr was helping on the compound, Sister Freda said to her, "Come get in the car with me. I want to take you to the village. A widow lives there, and I've got to find money to build her a house. I've just *got* to."

When they arrived, Marilyn saw where the woman lived — a broken-down shelter with crumbling walls and a roof that had partially collapsed.

"Why, Sister Freda? Why do you feel you're the one to build her a house?" Marilyn queried.

"Because it's raining in on her — and there's nobody else to help her. We must minister to these people. Remember, James 1:27 tells us, 'We must care for widows in their troubles.' I'm just going to have to pray about this and trust God for the money."

How many times does Freda say, "I'm just going to have to pray about this and trust God"! In America we say the very same words, but we often say them casually. When the African uses that phrase it has greater depth of meaning, for God is often his only sufficiency to meet the crises he faces every day. Volunteer David Storm observed,

"These people have such astonishing faith. We in the West may have faith — but these people have to trust God for every single spoonful they put in their mouths."

MEDICAL AND DENTAL SLUM CLINICS

If the needs in the villages surrounding the hospital are great, the needs of those who live in the slums of Kipsongo, Tuwan and Matisi are even greater. These are people who can scarcely afford a meal, let alone medical care. Neglect is visible everywhere. Drinking polluted water and surviving on scavenged food that does not provide adequate nutrition, many suffer from skin infections and nearly all have worms. Lice and ringworm are also virtually universal. Epidemics that could have been prevented and diseases that could have been cured take their toll. Sister Freda cannot pass them by. Indeed, she approaches each patient with the utmost gentleness, the same whether he or she is a filthy street child or a wealthy donor. Her demeanor says, "You are the most important person in the world to me right now." Whenever she sets up a mobile clinic in one of these slums, the residents turn up in droves. No one has to announce their coming — long lines form in the twinkling of an eye, for to them the clinics are a godsend.

"LITTLE DAVID"
by David

When I was in Kenya I went with Sister Freda when she conducted one of her clinics in a slum area. Taking a doctor with her, and often enlisting the help of visiting nurses, she listens intently to the needs of the people who come to her, and does everything in her power to help.

While I was observing and helping as I could, a young boy in a ragged T-shirt came up to me. The boy put his hand on his chest — almost as if saluting. I returned the "salute." But the boy didn't smile. In fact, he stood out among the other children because he *didn't* smile. The boy said something in Swahili, and I asked one of the Kenyan pastors to interpret.

"This boy wants you to feel his ribs, David."

I gently placed my hand on the boy's chest. I was shocked to feel the bones that almost protruded through the skin. From the pained look on his face,

I knew he needed to see a doctor quickly and took him to Sister Freda.

A brief examination by the doctor confirmed the seriousness of the injury. "This boy needs X-rays right away." But before arrangements could be made, his mother whisked him away. Search as we might, "Little David," as everyone nicknamed him, could not be found anywhere. For days we tried to locate him in the surrounding areas, but to no avail.

Why did Little David not get help? Because his father had beaten him severely, and his mother was afraid that the police would get involved if she allowed him to get medical care. To this day, the memory of the young boy haunts me. How many other "Little Davids" are there? It's a question that keeps Sister Freda praying and working night and day.

The stories of these two women provide a glimpse of the scope of need in the slums:

- Mary grimaced in pain. One week before, her right arm was broken in a domestic brawl. A kind neighbor wrapped the arm in a piece of cloth to support it, which allowed Mary to use her left hand to attend to her four children and do her household chores. Mary had no intention of looking for medical help, for she had no money to pay. The best she could hope for was that, in time, the painful arm would heal on its own. But a staff member from Sister Freda's medical clinic found her in Kipsongo, gave her treatment, and renewed courage to go on.

▪ How long would you put up with a toothache before going for help? Not as long as Margaret had waited. Because of prolonged tooth decay her jaw was swollen and her face disfigured. She had been in agonizing pain for many long weeks, hoping against hope that help would come from somewhere. Then one day Sister Freda set up a mobile clinic in her very neighborhood, and with the clinic came relief for Margaret and many others like her.

In the midst of the overwhelming privation of those who live in the slums, Sister Freda and her staff experience the blessing of seeing faces of despair and misery change to faces of hope and gratitude.

BRICK-AND-MORTAR DENTAL CLINIC

According to a CNN report , there is only one dentist in Kenya for every 60,000 people.[1] Treating dental patients in a mobile clinic is at best, difficult. Sister Freda has long yearned to be able to meet this dire need on her compound.

You can imagine her joy when Rich Kofron offered to set up a dental treatment center within the very walls of her medical center.

THE DENTAL CLINIC
by Rich

While many travel to Kenya to go on "Safari" to see exotic animals in their natural habitat, we had a mission: to visit Sister Freda, this humble nurse who, for more years than she would want me to mention, has dedicated her life to the care of the less fortunate — and to bring with us the answer to a long-standing prayer of hers.

With faith as big as Mt. Kenya, Sister Freda had been praying since 1999 that God would someday provide the resources to add a dental clinic to her medical center. Seven years later her desire was fulfilled; Sister Freda now has a dental operatory and a load of supplies and instruments that my wife, Sherry, and I felt blessed and honored to be able to personally hand-deliver to her.

As we unpacked the suitcases full of instruments and supplies and arranged them on the top of a desk, Sister Freda cried tears of joy. She was as excited as a child on Christmas morning. A local dentist who will now volunteer in the clinic every Friday was on hand, ready to see our first group of patients. But before we treated patients, Sister Freda insisted that we hold hands around the desk and thank God for this long-awaited day.

Do you and I have a faith that waits patiently for six or seven years? At the time of our visit the balance of the equipment and supplies were still in a ship's container, waiting to be released to the hospital (more patience, I guess), but that didn't stop us from seeing patients. With my trusty Mini Mag Lite, mask, gloves, tongue depressor, and wheelchair for the patient, I perched on the edge of the desk, and assisted Doc as he began seeing patients, sixteen in all that afternoon, with a total of eighteen extractions.

With a dental clinic and X-ray equipment set up at the hospital, slum dwellers like Margaret, whose festering tooth progressed into a major medical problem, can come and be treated promptly. What Rich Kofron began, others are developing further, so that in the future dentists can come and begin work immediately.

VISION CARE

Sister Freda has long conducted simple eye tests and dispensed donated glasses, for which disadvantaged people are very grateful. But in Kitale there has not been a single optometrist to prescribe custom-made glasses, a frustration to Sister Freda. Even if someone had money to pay for the glasses, one must travel to Eldoret or Nairobi to be fitted.

Hearing of Sister Freda's work in Kenya and her concern for those who so badly needed eye care, Dr. Rob Henslick, an optometrist in Laguna Niguel, California, made the decision to help. In 2007 he came to Kitale, bringing with him 500 pairs of glasses, donations from large U.S. manufacturers of frames and eye medications — more than $40,000 worth — and all the equipment needed to set up an optometry clinic at the Medical Center. Sister Freda was elated.

"Dr. Rob," as he likes to be called, held vision clinics not only at the Center but also in the rural areas surrounding Kitale. In the outlying areas, where he did not have optometric equipment available, at first Dr. Rob used the familiar acuity (vision) chart to determine what strength of glasses a person needed. But he ran into difficulty in determining whether the person could not see the chart well or whether the problem was that he or she could not read.

Not to be thwarted, Dr. Rob discovered that a common Kenyan bracelet that is about an inch wide and covered with patterns of brightly colored beads would stand in nicely for a Western eye chart. He would have the patient look at the beads at various distances, and when the person smiled, Dr. Rob knew the patient could see them clearly. "But even bigger is the smile that lights up a person's face," notes Dr. Rob, "when he is finally fitted with glasses and can see clearly for the first time in perhaps thirty years."

Dr. Rob's hope was to find an optician (the person who grinds lenses and fits glasses) in Kitale who could work with him. But no one could be found. Imagine his surprise, then, when on the last day of his time in Kenya, he arrived at the hospital to find an optician already set up on the compound, busily testing eyesight. Introducing himself, Dr. Rob learned that Stephen was a believer from Nairobi who, unbeknown even to Sister Freda, had been coming periodically to various locations in Kitale to test eyesight.

When Dr. Rob asked if on his next visit the optician from Nairobi would like to be taught how to use the new optometric equipment, he responded excitedly in the affirmative. Dr. Rob will obtain donated lenses for the clinic, and, much to Sister Freda's delight, Stephen has the ability to grind them at low cost, putting them into donated frames. As soon as this plan can be put into effect, even the poor will be able to afford prescription glasses.

Dr. Rob expressed how inadequate he felt to meet the tremendous needs of the people. "When I started a clinic at eight o'clock in the morning, eighty people would already be in line, having come from miles away. And yet they would continue to come," he recounted. Having worked as fast as he could without stopping for lunch, at the end of the day there might still be forty people in line who had to be turned away, after they had waited for hours. Sister Freda has been heard to comment, "*Now* you will believe how bad things are. No one believes how bad things are." She is overjoyed that, now Dr. Rob has "seen" the need, he comes twice a year to Kitale, and enlists other optometrists to come as well.

CIRCUMCISION CARE

Another unusual service that Sister Freda offers to the young men of the slums and the streets is circumcision care. In some Kenyan tribes circumcision is delayed until young manhood. Sister Freda performs the operations and then follows up with return visits for a free checkup and redressing.

In Kenya's forty-two tribes, the method of male circumcision varies widely. Some tribes circumcise baby boys, others don't. The Maasai, for example, still circumcise young men over the age of eighteen who pass into manhood with a traditional ceremony. Before the rite, the boys spend months in the bush with wild animals. In times past a boy was required to kill a lion with a spear and bring back the mane as proof of his manhood, but now Maasai are permitted to kill lions only if their cattle are being attacked.

The circumcision procedure is done by a man using a traditional knife — the same knife is used on several young men — followed by application of traditional medicine (moist grass and cow manure boiled and made into a poultice) to heal the wounds: very painful. Some die from excessive bleeding, infection, tetanus, or pneumonia. Different tribes circumcise their boys at different times; for instance, in Western Kenya it is common to circumcise in August of leap year. I spoke with one man who told me that the rite was celebrated with a party for him and his friends; everyone at the party had fun except him!

OUTREACH TO THE TRIBAL PEOPLE

When I asked Sister Freda how the ethnic clashes that occurred in Kenya during the late 1980s and early 1990s had affected the people she works with, she explained that the violent tribal clashes had displaced many families, who had run from their homes and settled along the swampy farms neighboring the hospital property in Birunda. As outcasts, the refugee families live in pathetic conditions. At an altitude of 6000 feet, their makeshift houses lack adequate walls and roofs, providing little protection from the cold. Consequently, all the diseases that plague the poor of Africa attack these families and their children with vigor.

It's an uphill task for Sister Freda to take medical services to so many families. The solution has been to set up mobile clinics that can be moved from village to village. Additionally, she and Richard help the people rebuild their "*manyattas*," (temporary shelters of twigs, mud and cow dung constructed by the village women) to withstand the heavy rains.

The Medical Center serves as a kind of emergency room or trauma center for victims of tribal conflicts. Sister Freda was working at the hospital one day when a man was brought in who had terrible machete cuts all over his head, some of them quite deep. He was a member of a minority tribe that is low on the "totem pole" of the African social order and had been banned from the area by another tribe. Just a mile from the hospital compound, warfare had broken out between the tribes, resulting in the man's terrible wounds.

As it happened, one of Sister Freda's nurses was shopping with her baby in this area at the time of the attack. In the midst of the tribal conflict, mother and baby were arrested and taken to the local women's prison. Sister Freda met with the authorities to obtain their release. Beyond treating medical problems, Sister Freda's work extends to advocacy for those in need, regardless of class or station in life.

Poor living conditions of the Kenyan tribal peoples result in meningitis and diarrheal diseases, along with tuberculosis. Add to all these problems the rise of HIV/AIDS, and you have obstacles that would cause a lesser person than Sister Freda to give up and go back to the comfortable life her nursing skills could provide. I observed that she is resolutely motivated by Jesus' command: "Love your neighbor as yourself," Galatians 5:14.

Sister Freda has her hands more than full with the needs of the tribes who live around her in Birunda and Kitale. But she has not stopped there. That is why she was so pleased when Dr. Terry Hodges, dentist, and Dr. David Haymes, internist, both volunteers from Dallas, Texas, agreed to go with her to conduct clinics among the tribes of northern Kenya.

"Outstanding in my mind," recalled Dr. Hodges, "is the dental clinic we conducted in a tribal area in the north. We chose a location down by a river. No one was around as we set up our card table and laid out instruments and medicines. But very quickly 200–300 people appeared out of nowhere. Using the large root of a banyan tree for a dental chair, I began to extract teeth, with Dr. Haymes as my anesthesiologist.

"It's impossible to do dental reconstruction at a clinic like this," explained Dr. Hodges. "Our goal is pain relief through extractions." And extract teeth they did! Sister Freda supplied the only needles she had — the large size normally used for blood extraction. And they had no topical anesthesia.

"We treated people of all ages, from a woman who was eighty to ninety years old down to a two-year-old child. Not a one so much as made a wry face when we injected the anesthesia — not a single negative reaction, though I knew the injections, especially in the palate, were painful."

On the occasions when she visits the West and East Pokot regions of Kenya, which are not far from the border of Uganda and Sudan, Sister Freda never ceases to be struck by the lack of basic facilities — schools, hospitals, churches, roads, telephones — the list goes on and on.

Located on the border of Sudan, the Kakuma refugee camp is one of the oldest and largest in the world. Housing 100,000 people, the camp's inhabitants — miserable as they are — at least have the barest of essentials for survival. Tribal people living beyond the Kakuma refugee camp, however, are often far worse off than those in the camp.

People who live in these remote communities undergo so many hardships that it is easy to think, suggests Sister Freda, that nothing good can come out of these areas. Temperatures reach 120° Fahrenheit and the mosquitoes torment. Yet, Sister Freda points out, it is here that one finds the real culture of

Africa — unchanged by any western influence. God's work-manship is evident in the landscape — the hills and valleys, rocks and trees, even the herds of cattle who are raised by the nomadic tribes who populate the region. She is impelled to do what she can to ease their suffering.

Sister Freda tells of one visit to Lomut in Sigor, which is in the Rift Valley:

> Our 4-wheel-drive Toyota Prado reels with pain as we navigate the difficult terrain. We are on our way to the center of the village, where we will set up a medical clinic. We pass by many of the people who are walking to the clinic. The presence of a car on their roads is a remarkable thing. Some of them have grown up without ever seeing one, and they run along-side at their fastest speed, astonished to see that it is running faster than they can run. We are sorry we cannot give them a lift, but they are not annoyed. Their joy is that they can get free medical attention, and they will walk and run many miles to get this God-sent gift.
>
> As we travel along we do not come across any school, except the one where we are setting up the center. Schools in this part of Kenya are so rare. And when you find one, it has no infrastructure at all. The best and most common facilities are huge trees that provide shade and serve as a classroom. Big stones or logs are used for desks and chairs. The ground is used as a chalkboard by the teachers and as a writing

book by the pupils. Illiteracy, especially among girls, is very high.

Here we learn that the outdated cultural rite of female circumcision (mutilation) is rampant. Girls as young as twelve years of age are circumcised and immediately married off to suitors known only to their parents. Health risks go with the practice, including bleeding to death, contracting infections such as HIV/AIDS, and long-term effects on childbirth.

In these nomadic districts, the child mortality rate is very high. Many factors are responsible, including poor health care before and after birth, births conducted at home and without professional help, no child immunization programs, and malnutrition.

We are late arriving for the medical clinic because of the bad roads, but because the people are so needy, we treat them without taking a rest. We are nevertheless conscious that we must leave before dusk for Marich Pass, the camp where we will spend the night, because of security. Frequent spates of cattle rustling take place here, and we must not be caught by one, or both our medical work and our own safety will be in danger.

With the assistance of a local interpreter, we learn of the myriad of health and social problems that face these people. Malaria and malnutrition are very common. New mothers are brought to us with childbirth complications due to female circumcision. Newborn babies suffer from tetanus because the traditional

> midwives use cow dung to seal the umbilical cord.
> Excessive bleeding during childbirth and circumcision
> leads to infections. Typhoid fever and other diseases
> are prevalent due to contaminated water. The list
> never seems to end!
>
> Ancestral gods play a great part in the life of Pokot
> communities, and churches in this area are rare. Our
> clinics therefore bring a preacher, who will tell them
> of the true God, the One who is greater than the
> gods of Mount Mtello.

The Sabaots of the Mt. Elgon area and the Pokots traditionally believed that their god was somewhere in the mountains or in the sea. They had special men, elders, who prayed to these gods for blessings, such as for rain in times of prolonged drought. Even now some tribes have witchdoctors to whom they go for help, and they say that it works.

Sister Freda continues,

> There is so much we need to do. We need advocacy
> for young girls in order to put a stop to the dehu-
> manizing practice of female circumcision. We need
> to increase our rounds for the medical clinics and to
> provide food relief for the famine-stricken families.
> But above all, we need to preach Christ to the people.

"The harvest is plentiful but the workers are few. Ask the Lord of the harvest, therefore, to send out workers into his harvest field," Matthew 9:37–38.

chapter 6

IN CRISIS

Besides Nairobi and its surrounding area, hardest hit in the violence that broke out following the December 2007 election was western Kenya, which includes the area where Sister Freda lives and works.

Because the skirmishes went on ruthlessly for weeks in slums, villages, town centers, and on roads and highways, many people came to the Medical Center for help. The staff treated burn cases, stab wounds, and machete wounds, as well as those with diseases such as acute diabetes who had not been able to take their medication with them when they fled.

Also treated were many who were suffering with acute depression as the result of the trauma they had experienced. Sister Freda wrote:

> In Kakamega District a man was found hanging on a rope because he had lost all of his family members during the clashes. Last week villages on Mt. Elgon [Kenya's second highest peak] were on fire. Everyone who was of the wrong tribe lost everything —

all the years of hard labor went up in flames. People fled from the mountain on foot with few or no earthly possessions, only their lives having been spared.

Refugee camps were set up as safe places for those who had no place to go. But the sheer numbers made living conditions miserable. Sister Freda described the situation at one of the camps:

> When we arrived at Kachibora Refugee Camp we saw rows of very small tents [actually, tarpaulins provided by the Red Cross] which each sheltered up to seven family members. Entering the tents, we saw dusty flea-infested floors. Women, children and men sleep on the bare ground. When it rains, the dust turns to mud. Many women and children were lined up for the precious commodity of water, which was brought by a Red Cross tanker. This water was not enough for the over 20,000 people living in the camp.
>
> We spoke with one woman who was seven months pregnant when the attacks came. With a toddler on her chest and another on her back and two young ones at her side, she ran nonstop to the center— only to have a miscarriage a few days later. A 56-year-old widow fled with her nine children after their house was torched and all her sheep and goats perished. She thanked God for the miracle of life.[1]

According to Sister Freda, Kachibora Refugee Camp was only one example of dire circumstances for those seeking a place of safety.

> We held another clinic by a church refugee sanctuary where there are more than 600 men, women and children, and their only shelter is the church. No bedding, no clothes, no food.[2]

In subsequent communications, she continued:

> At the refugee camps, things are going from bad to worse. The women and young children are being raped by men who are infected with HIV. The HIV-positive men, women and children have no access to ARVs (antiretroviral meds) and limited access to any health care. The women who ran with only the clothes on their backs have no change of clothes, and if they had their menstrual periods, their clothes are blood-stained. They do not even have water to shower. Sadness and sorrow is on their faces as they wonder when calm is going to return.

> The food ration is inadequate and many women and children do not have a balanced diet as they can eat only what is offered. The other day I took some bananas to the children, and up to three were sharing one banana. They have learned to wait patiently for the little that is offered, no fighting or jostling for

> food. I feel so sorry for them that I shed tears. This
> being the dry season, all the grass has dried up. The
> camps are very dusty, making them fertile ground for
> jiggers. Most people in the camps have no footwear,
> and their feet are now infected. You can see little
> children walking as if they are crippled, because of
> the jiggers in and between their toes.

Probably no creature on earth can cause as much torment for its size as the tiny jigger, a six-legged larva that attacks in low, damp areas. Jiggers (not the same as "chiggers," found in the southern U.S.) do not burrow into the skin, but insert their mouthparts in a skin pore or hair follicle, injecting a digestive fluid that disintegrates skin cells so they can be used as food. A feeding "tube" formed by the jigger secretion and skin cells permits the jigger to extract food. Over the next two weeks 100 eggs are released and fall to the ground, perpetuating the chances of infection. Their bites produce small reddish welts on the skin accompanied by intense itching. If not removed they can cause infection, deformity, loss of limb — even death from secondary infections. When needles used to remove them are shared, transmission of the HIV virus can occur.[3]

But jiggers, even though responsible for serious medical problems, are "minor" compared with the other dilemmas the people face. Talking to the refugees, Sister Freda learned:

> Few of them want to return to their homes as they
> have lost everything they owned. One of them, an
> old man of 85, was milking his cow when the enemy

struck. He was told to leave or die. As he walked a few meters away, he looked back and saw his house and maize store burning and the men walking away with the old man's one cow.

This past week another church was burned near Eldoret and many people lost their lives. As they fled others suffered severe injuries from arrow wounds. The arrows can't be pulled out as they are barbed, which means the people require surgery, sometimes major operations.

What can be done for these "internally displaced persons," as the government calls them, poses a huge challenge. Some have already gone back to their home areas, but others are too afraid, for the very people who killed their loved ones and destroyed their properties are still in their neighborhoods. Yet others are too traumatized by what they witnessed to go back.

Then there are the orphans. When Sister Freda commented to Pastor Steve Rutenbar, "There's a real opportunity for ministry in Cherengani Hills Refugee Camp," she was making an understatement. When she took Pastor Steve to the camp, he found 22,000 people living in tents on just less than an acre of land — with only five latrines. Furthermore, they learned there were 6,000 kids separated from their parents — "tiny kids wandering through the camp crying out for their mommies and daddies," Steve observed, heartbroken. Homes must be found for these traumatized children or they will most certainly face life as street children, thieves and prostitutes.

The arson, rape and killings lasted more than six weeks. But the heartache and scars will last for a lifetime. Sister Freda told me she is very worried by what effect life in refugee camps will have on the young. She sees the terrible, vacant look on their faces — the look of, "I have lost everything. Life is not worth living."

Sister Freda is doing her part to give hopeless people a reason to live. Her Medical Center is open 24 hours daily, and all the sick and injured receive the same care no matter which tribe they belong to. In her house, in the feeding program, and at the clinic, only Swahili and a little English are spoken to minimize tribal differences. As long as she has supplies, Sister Freda will continue to conduct clinics and distribute aid at the six refugee camps within her reach.

One thing is certain — Sister Freda will surely be on her knees asking God's help:

> I rely on God 100%, as usual, and even more now than before. I had only seen war on television and read about it in books, but I had never experienced it like now.

> The war in Kenya, my own country, has taught me to pray more, to love my neighbor, and above all, to love the Lord our God, with all my body, might and my soul. So we humble ourselves here, waiting for God to repair our damaged country and heal our broken hearts.

Bringing Hope
to Women and Children

When Sister Freda sees women who have no shoes, whose feet are infected by jiggers so that they can't walk properly, she is torn by both sadness and anger. "The frustration," she says, "drives me to my knees as I pray unceasingly day and night."

Sister Freda's own painful experience in a forced marriage gave her special compassion for the plight of Kenyan women, particularly village women. For these women in the countryside, life is much more difficult than it is for women living in cities. They are forever in search of food, firewood and water — all the while carrying babies on their backs. The rivers are far away, often a two-hour walk, and firewood is very scarce. In the cities women have a chance for education, better paying jobs, and a better life. While the average life expectancy in Kenya is 48.93 years,[1] tragically, women in some areas can expect to live only 35 years.

Traditionally, girls are denied the right to education, and the right to choose whom they will marry, and many are forced to submit to female circumcision before marriage. The male reasoning behind the practice of female circumcision is that after this procedure the woman will no longer experience pleasure in sexual relations, and so will not be tempted to be unfaithful. In some cases the young girls submit willingly, because they will have difficulty finding a man who will marry them if they do not. In other cases, the procedure is done forcibly. The practice is maintained "officially" by only a few tribes (Kalengin, Pokot, and Maasai), and more prevalently in the bush. For those girls whose cultures still insist on the procedure, the ordeal is devastating, often resulting in excessive bleeding, infection, tetanus, and sometimes death. Complications at childbirth caused by the practice sometimes require surgery and certainly increase the pain suffered.

Although outlawed for girls under the age of eighteen by Parliament's passage of the Children's Act law in 2001, Minister of State for Home Affairs Linah Jebii Kilimo says the practice of female genital mutilation is still widespread. She estimates that "Thirty-eight percent of Kenyan women have undergone FGM [female genital mutilation], the figure soaring to eighty or ninety percent among girls in some of the more rural districts."[2]

A HEART FOR CHILDREN

Jesus said, "I tell you the truth, whatever you did for one of the least of these . . . you did for me."

Matthew 25:40

Sister Freda has quite a way with children. When she was visiting in the United States and having dinner with a group of us at the home of John and Sandi West, their grandson, who had never in his life seen Sister Freda, came in the front door and walked straight to her with both arms raised. She is like a magnet to children, for they sense her love for them.

Jana O'Guin saw Sister Freda's concern for children on a visit to the women's prison in Kitale, where Jana was teaching Celebrate Recovery, a Christian 12-step program for those with addictions. About a dozen children were there with their mothers in prison, for mothers are allowed to have their children with them in detention until the children are four years old.

One woman insistently tried to give Jana her little boy — for keeps. Jana didn't know what to do, so she asked Sister Freda for direction.

"Oh, take him, take him!" said Sister Freda.

The boy's father was married to another woman, not his mother. Jana talked to the prison authorities, who said, "No," but Jana can't help wondering what her husband would have said if she had unexpectedly gotten off the plane with a little boy to join their family. She is certain of one thing: Sister Freda would have been very happy.

In addition to Sister Freda's five children from her first marriage, Emma, Michael, Erick, Stella and Frank, she and Richard have adopted several and provide care and education for many, many more, including several of her own grandchildren. Counting their children will always be an impossibility — the number is now more than one hundred, some of them married, some already grandparents. One comes to the conclusion that if there were no physical and financial limitations, Sister Freda would welcome every needy child who comes. Richard has a special relationship with these children as well, bonding with them in a way that is beautiful to see.

Let me tell you the stories of just a few.

▪ MOSES

You already read how baby Moses' life was saved when he was found in the tall grass that the caretaker was slashing with his machete. Sister Freda asked Fruited Plains, a ministry headed by Mike and Michele Robison, to find someone to sponsor or adopt baby Moses. When Mischa and Matt McGill, who live in California, saw Moses' picture, a deep concern for him was born in their hearts. Until someone adopts him, Sister Freda is overseeing his care and the McGills are providing for his support.

▪ ESTHER

Esther was brought to Sister Freda by an old woman from the bush who said she was the grandmother. The child was about eight months old and weighed only nine pounds. In addition to malnutrition, she had malaria that had to be treated immediately if she was to survive. Esther's mother was mentally deranged. Because she had drowned Esther's eight-year-old sister, the villagers took Esther from her so she would not suffer the same fate.

Esther's mother had kept her bound to her back, with her legs raised up over her head for so long that they were frozen in that position — the pose of a baby born in breach position.

The "grandma" who brought her to Sister Freda left with the heartrending comment, "If you can save her, save her. But if it's not possible, it's all right."

Sister Freda and the staff began to care for little Esther, giving her long months of patient therapy and rehabilitation. Eventually she was able to straighten her legs and learn to walk — by jumping with both feet instead of taking steps. In fact, she learned so well that the hospital staff got plenty of exercise running to catch up to her.

Esther loves music and responds greatly to it. Not only can she talk, she also loves to imitate her schoolteacher, dramatically pointing to the blackboard — "This is capital 'A,' and this is small 'a.'" Bright and adorable!

■ DAVIS

A mother came to the hospital seeking medical care, bringing with her her one-year-old son, a darling boy named Davis. She was an alcoholic, a member of the Sabaot tribe, from the area of Mt. Elgon. This mother left the hospital without Davis, abandoning him to whatever fate might be his. Dismayed that a mother could just walk away from her child, Sister Freda cared for him for two years without outside financial help. Now that he is ready to begin primary school, a Colorado couple is providing for his support and education.

■ MORGAN

On a missions trip to Kenya in 2006, Theresa Loza and her son Broc were visiting the slum area of Milamani, when they

A village house like the one in which Sister Freda grew up.

How village women now carry water to their homes.

Looking with faith at the future Nursing Academy.

Dispensing medication.

Sister Freda's Medical Center

A mother who walked 5 miles for treatment.

Both mother and child are being treated for malaria.

Reaching out with compassion and help.

Treating a mobile clinic patient.

Sister Freda and Pastor John pray for a sick Kipsongo woman.

"I saw Sister Freda debride [remove the dead skin from] a six year-old girl's burned hand so tenderly and carefully that the girl did not cry. Then Sister Freda held her closely in her lap for several minutes and then gave her a softdrink."
– Dr. David Haymes, Houston, TX

Kipsongo mother and child.

Kipsongo girl wearing her best dress.

Typical Kipsongo home.

"With my new glasses I can see that now!"

Dr. Rob uses a Kenyan beaded bracelet for his "eye chart" when his patients cannot read.

Under Sister Freda's care, Morgan is no longer malnurished.

Chapter 7, "Bringing Hope to Women and Children," tells the stories of these children. See pages 82-90.

A boy from Sister Freda's school.

Sister Freda and Harold Sala holding (L-R) Morgan, Moses, Esther, and Davis.

The feeding program and education bring smiles to otherwise destitute children.

Children at Oasis of Hope receive Sister Freda's tender care.

The leaders at Oasis of Hope consult with Sister Freda on the children's nutrition - and it shows!

Sister Freda treats the children at Oasis of Hope's Children Center.

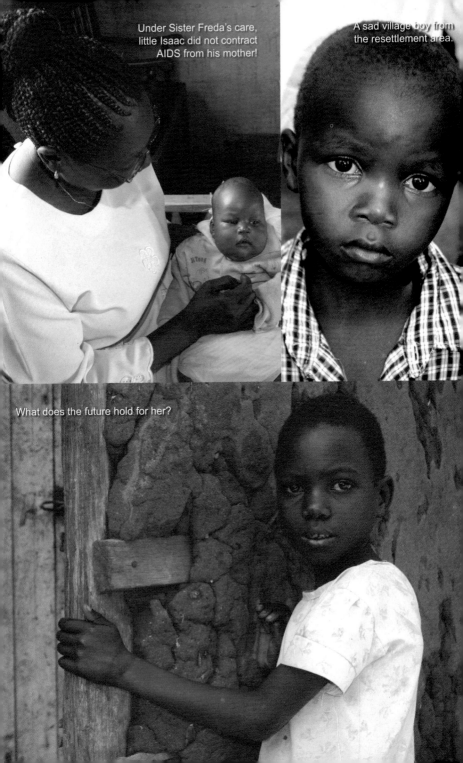

Under Sister Freda's care, little Isaac did not contract AIDS from his mother!

A sad village boy from the resettlement area.

What does the future hold for her?

spotted Morgan, an emaciated 18-month-old boy. They learned he was the son of Sammy, a former street boy, who was still in his teen years and caring for his son as best he could. Morgan's mom had abandoned him and was already married to someone else.

With Sammy's permission Theresa took the little curly-headed boy with her and began to nurture him. The first thing she noticed was that his diaper was red-brown. He was so hungry that he had been eating dirt. But soon she realized he was not only hungry but ill, and she brought him to Sister Freda.

Morgan, they discovered, was dehydrated and had malaria; at this young age he had pulmonary tuberculosis as well. Obviously he had to be admitted for treatment at the Medical Center.

Before Theresa left Morgan at the hospital — lying there so weak and sickly in a place that was strange to him, Morgan reached his little hand through the bed slats and placed it on Theresa's cheek — a silent "Thank you. I love you."

When he was healthy enough to leave the hospital, Sister Freda kept Morgan on her compound and provided for him. Because he was so malnourished, he had not yet learned to walk and used a "walking chair" to get around. But with gentle care and specialized treatment, he has grown strong. Little Morgan's heart is full of love because of the love he has received. A touching moment for Sister Freda was seeing Morgan ask to hold baby Moses on his lap — sharing the love that had been shown to him. He is now walking and running as well as any child his age.

■ LUCY

When Americans Mike and Michele Robison went to visit Endebess School, they brought some necklaces to give to the children. Almost before they knew it, they were surrounded, not only by the students but also by children from the streets who were not enrolled in the school.

While they were busy fastening the jewelry on the necks of the children, Michele accidentally dropped a few pieces. Out of the corner of her eye, she saw a small hand quickly pick them up. She figured whoever grabbed them would keep them, for street children take what they can get since they have almost nothing of their own.

Then Michele felt a gentle tap on her arm. When she looked down, a precious little girl with brown eyes was looking up at her. She held her hand out, and in it were the necklaces. Michele was amazed that this little girl, dressed in rags, had returned them, and her heart was instantly touched. Her name was Lucy, they learned. She had no family. Both parents were dead. When Michelle asked the teacher where Lucy lived, she responded, "It is not good."

That night Mike and Michele could not get Lucy's face out of their minds. Together they cried and prayed for her.

The next day Mike and Michele went back to see Lucy again. But she was gone. A boy in the school who knew where she was left to find her. After some time, they saw her walking up the road with a woman they did not recognize.

They learned that this woman was the one who had taken Lucy in to work, as little more than a slave, after Lucy's mother died. At age seven, Lucy was responsible for cooking, cleaning, fetching wood and water, and caring for a family of ten. She was not allowed to attend school. Beaten by various family members, she bore scars from the abuse she endured. Something had to be done!

The teacher and headmaster explained to the woman that Mike and Michele were there to help Lucy get into a school. The woman had no authentic claim to her, so quickly the Robisons helped Lucy into the van and left.

Mike and Michele could provide for Lucy's care and schooling at a boarding school. But where was she to live during the three one-month breaks that Kenyan children have when school is not in session?

"She will stay with Richard and me," said Sister Freda, firmly.

"No, Sister Freda. You can't do that. You already have so much to do. You're already caring for so many." Mike and Michele had not intended to burden Sister Freda with any more responsibility than she already bore.

But Sister Freda was persistent and not to be put off.

"It is decided, Michele. Lucy will stay with us when she is not in school." And that was final. So the arrangement was set. Mike and Michele would support Lucy, and to this day when Lucy is not in school, she lives with Richard and Sister Freda, secure in their love and care for her. The Robisons both knew their new "daughter" could not be placed with a more nurturing woman than Sister Freda. Michele says,

> I will always remember seeing Lucy in her new
> school uniform with Mike kneeling down, tying her
> shiny, new black school shoes. As soon as she put on

her uniform, she set off — armed with her new cup, bowl and spoon, ready for lunch with the other students at school.

We noticed, however, that she was walking oddly. She lifted her feet high with each step she took, like she was doing an awkward march.

"Do you know why she is walking like that?" Peter, our Kenyan driver, asked us.

"No, why?"

"Because she never had shoes before."[3]

Why would Sister Freda take Lucy in? She was already raising two of her own grandchildren. She didn't know Mike and Michele. She didn't know Lucy. The only conclusion that can be deduced is that she did so because she cares.

The stories of children Sister Freda has rescued and cared for could fill an entire book. When all of these children become capable, functioning adults, it will surely be because they are graduates of Sister Freda's School of Compassion.

"Sometimes in the mornings I just don't feel like getting up," Sister Freda told me, "until I remember all that I have planned to do during the day, and then I force myself to get up. When I see a smile of thanks on a child's face, I know the day has been worth getting up for."

Experts tell us Kenya has 1.7 million orphans, most of them as a result of AIDS, and that figure is projected to rise to 2.4 million by 2010.[4] The reality that Sister Freda cannot help them all does not keep her from making a life-changing difference to those God brings across her path.

chapter 8

In Times of Discouragement

As I write about Sister Freda, who truly has a "heart of compassion and hands of care," I'm concerned not to convey that she is more an "angel" than a real person. (Although I did once tell her, "Freda, you qualify for sainthood in every way — except that you haven't died yet!") I asked her to tell me about the struggles she faces.

The first that came to her mind was the problem of paying local doctors, who want their money on the spot when they come to see a patient, charging as much as $75 for treatment. "Sometimes I don't have it, so I have to sell some vegetables, or even a cow, to get the money.

"Then there are the taxes." The words now poured out without a pause. "Some patients come, stay a long time, and leave owing half a million shillings, with no way to pay. You see, whether or not the patients pay their bills, I have to pay taxes on the money they owe me. The only way I can avoid the taxes is by writing off their debts quickly. But then I can never collect on those debts.

"Another problem is that some nurses are looking only for a job, not a ministry." She went on to explain, "Perhaps a nurse is operating her own clinic on the side and needs instruments or supplies or medicines. So she takes a blood pressure cuff or a surgical instrument or some pills with her when she leaves the hospital. I need a reliable full-time administrator who will keep a daily accounting of what we have."

I had the feeling that all of these problems had been building up inside, and Sister Freda needed someone to talk to about them.

> And there's the road. From the main highway to the hospital is a distance of nearly two miles. As you have seen, the road is just red dirt. When it rains, sometimes we have to abandon our vehicle and walk to the compound in the downpour, because the potholes are too deep and the mud too slick for us to keep the car on the road.

> Providing sufficient salaries for nurses is a nightmare. Then there are the chemists [pharmacies]. At one time I [Freda] owed 200,000 shillings [nearly $3000] to chemists all over town, and I had run out of credit to buy any more medicines. Sandy Jackson, a friend from Houston, was visiting me. Sandy was in the cottage praying earnestly for the money, when American Roger Barnett's vehicle appeared. I was running from the hospital to the cottage when he handed me a

> zippered pencil case and said he was leaving the country. I handed the unopened case to Sandy, said goodbye to him, and quickly went back to the hospital. Later that day Sandy and I decided we'd better open the case and see what was inside. $5,000! We both cried and then we prayed a prayer of thanksgiving to God. The next day Richard was very busy chasing our debts all over town — and there was enough remaining to pay the salaries.

Clearly God is the first Person to whom Sister Freda turns for help when times are tough.

"We are faced with children who have passed their exams very well and want to go to high school, but school fees are very expensive, and we also want to help out with their books, and uniforms," she says. "Somehow through prayer we manage. When we get little handouts, we share — whether the gift be food, clothing, money or medicine."

Distressing to her since the 1980s has been losing so many people to HIV/AIDS. "The dreaded disease leaves behind widows, orphans and destitutes," Sister Freda says sadly, and you can read a certain despondency in her face. She is always wishing she could do more.

Sometimes the problems for Sister Freda seem to pile up as high as the mountains surrounding Kitale, and discouragement weighs her down. She specifically mentions, "jealous doctors, lazy staff, immature matrons, missing supplies, insufficient school staff, a worn-out vehicle . . . ," but adds, "Then when I remember that Jesus went through trials, I realize this is normal."

When she feels like she can't take another step, Sister Freda turns to one of her favorite Scriptures — Psalm 121, for help to go on:

> I lift up my eyes to the hills —
>   where does my help come from?
> My help comes from the LORD,
>   the Maker of heaven and earth.
>
> He will not let your foot slip —
>   he who watches over you will not slumber;
> indeed, he who watches over Israel
>   will neither slumber nor sleep.
>
> The LORD watches over you —
>   the LORD is your shade at your right hand;
> the sun will not harm you by day,
>   nor the moon by night.
>
> The LORD will keep you from all harm —
>   he will watch over your life;
> the LORD will watch over your coming and going
>   both now and forevermore.

At present Sister Freda's Medical Center is staffed by consulting doctors, two clinical officers, six nurses, and six nurse's aides. In addition, there are several support staff, a pharmacist, and a lab technician.

Electricity has only recently been brought to the property. In 1998 a payment of 180,000 shillings (more than $2,700) was made to pay for the lines to be brought in from a mere half mile away. But after numerous trips to Kenyan Power and Lighting Company in Eldoret, nothing happened and the file mysteriously disappeared from the government office.

Sister Freda says at one time they were told that they could have electricity on the compound within twenty-four hours, for a payment of 2.4 million shillings ($36,000, an exorbitant price). So the center continued to buy gasoline for the water pump, diesel for power to operate the EKG machine, X-ray, dental and surgical equipment, and kerosene to light the lamps in the evenings — at a cost of 1,500 shillings (almost $25) a day. But now that the power lines reach the compound, an electric microscope can be used that sat inoperative under its dust cover for years because there was no electricity, replacing the microscope that had to be placed near a window so that the lab technician could see to use it. Much additional donated medical equipment requiring electricity can also be used. And the savings in costs will be considerable.

By the end of a day, Sister Freda is a failure at watching TV; a few minutes of television only serves as a sleep inducer after long days of responsibility.

Yet God supplies strength and courage to go on.

One morning before public power had been brought to the compound, Sister Freda and Marilyn Mohr arrived at the hospital to find that a woman had been admitted the night before, needing a Caesarean section. The surgery room was prepared, and the doctor arrived. Suddenly Sister Freda came running out of the hospital to Richard and Floyd, Marilyn's husband.

"We don't have fuel to run the generator for the operating theater. You men go and siphon some from our car's tank so that we can turn on the electricity!"

Was it a coincidence that Richard had just filled up the car with fuel that day? There was enough to enable them to finish the surgery.

DOING SO MUCH WITH SO LITTLE
by Jeanne and Dave

Sister Freda's Medical Center is truly out "in the sticks," for that is where she finds the people that she wants to reach. We traveled over miles of red dirt roads to find a crowd of people lined up to see the doctor at her compound — a doctor whose patients don't have money. Much of her equipment is antiquated; her surgery table looks like a patio lounge chair with metal legs. Yet, on this table hundreds of lives have been saved.

There isn't any washing machine to wash the linens. The clothes, towels and bed linens must be washed by hand in cold water with a scrub brush and handmade soap, then rinsed in two different tubs of water and wrung out by hand before being hung on clotheslines or laid over bushes to bleach and dry. Labor intensive but effective — this is how most laundry is done in Kenya.

Before we left, Sister Freda wanted our group, about twenty-five people, to come to the cottage on the compound to have refreshments. She insisted on serving each of us the food and drink she had prepared. No buffet-style eating here! She humbled us by serving us herself and making us feel like honored guests in her little cottage by the hospital. That night she visited us at the Conference Center and presented each of us with a gift, speaking a few kind words to each of us personally as she handed us her gifts.

Any limits Sister Freda may have in physical resources place no limits on the generosity of her heart.

The necessity of "making do" with whatever one has is quite foreign to most Americans in the medical field. Kathy Nielsen, an American career nurse, tells of a time when she was assisting in surgery at the Medical Center, and she decided to take a picture as the operation was taking place. After she took the shot, she set down her camera, pulled off her surgical gloves and tossed them in the trashcan. Then she donned a new pair before continuing surgery. If she needed to leave the room, she would throw away her used gloves and put on new ones when she came back in into surgery. All the time that this was going on, Kathy noticed one of Sister Freda's nurses eyeing her. The nurse couldn't believe that Kathy was actually throwing her gloves away.

A few days later Kathy was in the lab drawing blood from a patient who had malaria. She put the blood sample on the open window ledge to dry, because there was no electricity in the lab for a drying cabinet to dry the samples. As she did so, she glanced out the window. There, on a clothesline, were surgical gloves washed and hung out to dry. Then she understood why the Kenyan nurse had been watching her so incredulously. When you don't have an unending supply of gloves, used ones — even torn ones — are better than none at all.

Sister Freda would concur with Dr. David Stevens, who for years was on staff at Tenwek Hospital, a mission hospital located in another part of Kenya. Stevens once quipped, "Tell us what you need, and we will tell you how we've learned to get along without it."[1]

(In all fairness, thanks to donations, Sister Freda's Medical Center now has a more plentiful supply of surgical gloves, disposable needles, etc., though additional equipment and materials are always needed.)

chapter 9

THE BIG FOUR

As in most developing countries, four primary crises exist in Kenya today: disease, poverty, illiteracy and spiritual darkness. These are in addition, of course, to Kenya's specific political crisis of 2007. These four are challenges that drain the life-blood of the nation. Take a look at Sister Freda's part in making a difference in these areas.

1 THE CRISIS OF DISEASE

With preventative health care as her primary focus, Sister Freda has mounted an aggressive environmental health campaign. She teaches mothers how to care for their children — feeding, cleanliness, nutrition, even how to care for themselves. She takes pains to impress on them the importance of keeping appointments for their children's inoculations. When mothers give birth, the babies are given the first of these inoculations so there is no chance they will not receive this important protection because return visits were neglected. Sister Freda provides the same immunizations that are given to children in the U.S. — vaccines for poliomylitis, DPT, measles, tetanus, and anti-TB injections.

The poor of Kenya face almost overwhelming problems from malaria, typhoid, diarrheal diseases, pneumonia, meningitis, tuberculosis (from unpasteurized milk), brucellosis,[1] worms, and jiggers. In addition the poor must cope with malnutrition and serious burns from cooking on open fires. With her skills and compassion, Sister Freda's hospital and outpatient clinic, which can treat between two and four hundred patients a day, has brought hope to the poor. As part of the outpatient program, she offers family planning, inoculations, and nutrition counseling to the needy in the Kitale area.

WHAT ABOUT HIV/AIDS IN KENYA?

As in most countries where HIV/AIDS is rampant, Kenyans are reluctant to be tested. After all, what difference will it make if they know they are HIV-positive? They believe it to be a death sentence. They have no money for medicine, but even if they had the money, the latest medical treatments for HIV are not readily available except in the largest cities. Besides, these medications must then be taken for the rest of the person's life. Perhaps most painful is that if the community finds out they have AIDS, they risk being shunned. What many who are HIV-positive do *not* know is the importance of treating the infections that take advantage of the person's depressed immune system and thereby cut short their lives unnecessarily. Also not understood is the fact that unprotected sex is dangerous even for couples where both partners have the disease, because the virus can mutate into a more serious form.

Culture strongly affects the spread of AIDS in Africa. The practice of "grazing," — that is, having numerous partners even within marriage — multiplies the chances of contracting the disease. A widespread belief exists that if a man with AIDS will have sex with a virgin, he will be cured. It's not hard to see the risk this poses to little girls as young as four years old — and to boys as well — who are living on the streets.

Further contributing to the problem in western Africa is the custom of wife inheritance. Tradition has long dictated that when a man dies, his brother inherits his widow — also her house and land and animals. In previous generations, this practice was a good one that insured the family would be fed, clothed, sheltered, educated and protected. Convention frowned on the brother having sexual relations with her. But that taboo is no longer observed.

If the cause of the man's death was AIDS, which is now very probable, his widow no doubt also has the disease. When she becomes her brother-in-law's second wife, if he does not already have the disease, he too will contract AIDS and spread it to his first wife. In all probability, nine or ten months later, children will be born of both of those unions who will more than likely develop AIDS as well. The widow can scorn the tradition of coming the brother-in-law's second wife, but in doing so she and her children will probably find themselves homeless, driven from the community to face isolation and hunger — possibly even starvation.[2]

The distressing part of the prevalence of HIV/AIDS in Kenya, which has already cut life expectancy by twenty years,[3] is that it is preventable. The human skin is actually a strong barrier to the virus, for the AIDS virus will live only about three seconds on the surface of the skin. Only when there is a break in the skin allowing the transfer of body fluids does it infect a person — and then it is deadly.

Sister Freda treats the secondary infections of people who are HIV-positive with Bactrim or Septrim, but it is useless to put patients on expensive antiretrovirals unless they understand they must take them at the same time every day and can afford to stay on them, in all probability, the rest of their lives. On the encouraging side, she has found from experience that when people who are HIV-positive are given vitamins and good nutrition (beans, rice, *ugali*, lentils, fruits and vegetables, limiting their intake of meat, chicken, fish and eggs), they have a good quality of life and do very well for many years. Full-blown AIDS patients are referred to the AMPATH Clinic at the District (government) Hospital.

SHE UNDERSTANDS
by David and Kim

When I first came to Kenya and told Sister Freda I have had AIDS for 23 years, we immediately bonded. That was 2003. My wife, Kim, and I had been living in silence for more than thirteen years. But Sister Freda understood and accepted us immediately.

Having become infected with HIV from two units of contaminated blood that I had received following a motorcycle accident in 1983, I didn't even know I had the disease until symptoms showed up in 1992. Testing of blood supplies for HIV didn't begin until 1985. That my wife to this day does not test positive for HIV is a miracle in itself.

In 2003, when I went to Kenya for the first time, the issue was a very sensitive one for me. A few years before, the only pastor I had ever confided in had asked me to leave his church, instructing me to not even attend a small group. As a result, I was gun-shy of all pastors. But Pastor Steve not only encouraged me to go on the trip but also helped with all that was necessary to make it possible — even with such details as finding ice for transporting my meds.

The following year, Kim and I found ourselves back in Kenya heading an HIV/AIDS prevention ministry team. On our trips to Kenya we travel to churches and schools in different towns, teaching the facts about HIV/AIDS. One of our goals is to combat the pervasive misinformation and misunderstanding among Kenyans about the disease and how it is contracted. The fact that I have survived this long brings them hope.

Sister Freda is a woman who truly understands people who must live with this dread disease, for she deals with it every day. Approximately 6 percent of the population in Kenya have full-blown AIDS, say most experts.

Kim puts it so well,

Sister Freda has such a heart and bond with those who are sick. When I met her, I immediately felt her loving and caring concern for Dave. It was as though she herself was infected with AIDS, and knew or understood what it was like living with it. She made us feel so welcomed and so loved. Sister Freda really felt like a "sister," one who didn't judge and loves unconditionally.

> It is a joy to know we can have a positive influence in this needy part of the world by speaking out, breaking the stigma, shattering the silence, and dispelling the hurt.

KENYA'S #1 KILLER

You may be surprised to learn that malaria, not AIDS, however, is the #1 killer in Kenya. Studies indicate that malaria causes between 20 and 25 percent of all deaths, with up to 28 million Kenyans (70 percent of the population) being at risk, according to Britain's Department of International Development.[4] Approximately ninety children alone die daily of malaria in Kenya.[5]

Malaria is contracted from the bite of a malaria-infected mosquito, and the steps to contracting the disease are quite straightforward. When a mosquito bites an infected person, the insect ingests the malaria parasites found in the person's blood. The malaria parasite must grow inside the mosquito for a week or more before infection can be passed on to another person by the mosquito's bite. The parasites then travel to the "host's" liver (the liver of the person bitten by the mosquito), growing and multiplying there. Later they leave the liver and enter the red blood cells, still growing and multiplying. The red blood cells eventually burst, which allows the parasites to attack other red blood cells. If a mosquito bites this person while the parasites are still in his or her blood, this next mosquito will in turn ingest the parasites, which will grow, multiply, and begin the cycle all over again.[6]

There are four different types of malaria, but *Falciparum* is the most common one in northern Kenya — and the most dangerous. This form may go to the brain and produce cerebral malaria, causing coma and death if prompt treatment is not received. Yet in most cases of malaria, when Sister Freda begins treatment and sees that the person is hydrated, the patient recovers and can go home from the hospital by the second or third day.

Every year during the rainy season Sister Freda is confronted with severe cases of malaria due to the swampy environment and rampant mosquitoes. She once wrote me during the month of May, "It is malaria month now, and all hell has broken loose. We are spending a lot of money daily on medicines to help the poor who can't even afford to stay alive if not helped with medicines and care."

As with HIV/AIDS, prevention is the key. Because the mosquitoes that carry malaria bite between dusk and dawn, insecticide-treated bed nets can avert most of the danger.

INSPIRED BY SISTER FREDA
by Beth

Sister Freda told me that the most common problem she treats at the hospital is malaria — about 80 percent of the people who come to her are infected. As we saw her work and her ministry in the slum villages around Kitale, an idea was birthed in the heart of my husband, Kelly. Inspired by Sister Freda, we now have a ministry called Hope Span. Here is how it came about.

During our first visit to Kenya, when we would ask people, "What is your greatest need?" in addition to malaria medications, every person would say, "Mosquito nets!" So, our group took up a collection to purchase them at a cost of about $7 apiece. These nets will kill mosquitoes for a period of five years without harming the people. Then we decided to take our involvement one step further, and met with the owners of the company that is the largest producer of insecticide-treated mosquito nets in Africa. God gave us favor with them, and they agreed to sell us as many or few as we would need.

But who would distribute the nets — and do it fairly? At Pastor Steve's suggestion, we met with Rev. Stephen Mairori at ICM Seminary in Kitale about heading up the distribution. As it turned out, the seminary wives had been praying for over a year for a ministry project! A committee of seven women was formed to supervise net distribution and follow-up.

The nets are usually distributed by a local church in the village. As a result, new ties are established between the people and their church. The seminary wives and the pastor give the people the Gospel every time nets are distributed, and many respond. Churches have doubled in size as a result, and the health benefits have been remarkable. In the Mt. Elgon area there are villages that have had nets for two years and have not had ONE instance of malaria since they started using them!

There is no real cure for malaria. Once contracted, it remains dormant in a person's body. So, most sufferers contract malaria two or three times a year and, whenever they do, are so struck down that they can neither work nor tend to their families for several weeks at a time. Three hundred million people are infected every year — some say five hundred million, and every year three million of those die from the disease.[7]

Roughly 30 million pregnancies occur every year among women in malarious areas of Africa, yet less than five percent of pregnant women have access to effective interventions for malaria. For these women, the disease is a threat both to themselves and to their babies, with up to 200,000 newborn deaths each year as a result of malaria in pregnancy.[8]

This latter statistic was driven home to me when I was teaching in Mt. Elgon in 2006. I was heartbroken to learn that the daughter of my translator had recently lost a baby. The young mother had contracted malaria, and the unborn child died. Such unnecessary heartache!

Sister Freda's clinics distributed our very first mosquito nets, and she continues to give them out at her hospital. When she started the nursery school, she was adamant that the home of every child would have these special nets so that entire families can be spared the ravages of malaria. It is a joy to work with her in providing prevention instead of waiting until this feared disease strikes.

2 THE CRISIS OF POVERTY

The suffering of the poor in Kenya has a disconcerting, disquieting effect that can't be ignored. The dis-ease it leaves in your heart cannot be "switched off" like a T.V. program you don't like. It has a disturbing effect on your sense of emotional well-being.

Volunteer Theresa Loza will never be able to wipe from her memory what poverty can do to the human psyche. The setting was a churchyard in Kitale Town where she was helping with the feeding of people living on the streets. The woman next to her, who was holding her baby, had just been given a plate of food. All at once the baby reached out to grab her plate, knocking it to the concrete floor. The woman was irate, for her meal was now gone.

"The next thing I saw," recalls Theresa, "was a baby flying through the air and landing on the concrete floor, hitting its head on a wooden bench. I couldn't believe my eyes! I wanted to scream. Why had she thrown her baby down? Was she crazy? I tried to reach out to her, but she yelled at me and wouldn't let me help."

With the assistance of a translator, Theresa was shocked to learn that the mother had eaten almost nothing in the past month and was desperate for food — she was literally starving. Of course, she was given another plate of food. But Theresa's heart and mind will forever bear the imprint of the extreme desperation that poverty can bring.

How can even basic needs be met on an income of less than a dollar a day? Yet, this is what many Kenyans are trying to do.

Forty percent of the people are unemployed — not because they are lazy, but because there are no jobs available for them. (For example, the Medical Center's pharmacist, Agnes, had been working as a hairdresser to cover her expenses until hired by Sister Freda, because she could not find work in the area of her training.) Fifty-two percent of the population lives below the poverty level.

Attending a Sunday worship service at Deliverance Church in Kitale, I was stunned as the pastor told of a phone call he'd received from a fellow pastor of a rural church in the north of Kenya, where the drought was critical and famine severe. In desperation, the rural pastor's congregation had crowded into his small home, hoping to get at least one meal a day. But that week he had conducted the funerals of two of his members who died of starvation. Needless to say, the offering was generous that morning; the compassionate Kitale congregation also brought sacks of grain to the church to be taken to the hungry men and women.

Of course, wherever there is extreme poverty there is also increased crime. Sometimes stealing is explained away as "social justice" with the idea that "They have so much, and we have so little, so we're going to take some to even it out." Even Richard and Sister Freda, whose only goal in life is to relieve suffering and make life more bearable for the poor, have been attacked and robbed.

Thus, wherever possible, one of Sister Freda's desires is to help the poor have a source of income that will raise them from their poverty and all the painful problems that follow destitution. Sometimes volunteers can help her do this with their skills in developing small businesses. Her appreciation knows no bounds when she gets help from people skilled in this area.

AFTERNOON TEA
AT THE CHICKEN COOP
by Dean

I am an American who has been experimenting for some time now with building various types of chicken coops in Kitale; the goal is to find the best method for helping the people there to have eggs and broilers to sell so they can feed their families.

On one particular project eight Kenyans were helping me build a two-story chicken coop on Sister Freda's property. The whole process was a clash in cultures. The Type-A American working intensely to complete the work as quickly as possible — and the Kenyans working within their cultural framework of stopping for rest time, lunch, teatime, etc. It had been raining, and then the sun came out, making the working conditions steamy and miserable.

Enter Sister Freda with a substantial lunch and (expensive) bottled water — followed in a few hours by afternoon tea. She personally fed the crew for two days and then sent the men home with large baskets of pineapples, mangos, bananas, and other foods, along with gifts of scarves for their wives.

When the project was about three-fourths completed, she came just to see how it was going. There she stood in front of the chicken coop, crying — so amazed was she that people wanted to do this for her.

I used to work at my job 80 percent of the time and spend 20 percent of my time in missions. Then I began to pray that I could spend 20 percent of my time at my job and 80 percent of my time in world missions. When I changed my priorities, God blessed my company, doubling my work. And yet He has allowed me to be ever more deeply involved in reproducible self-sustaining micro-enterprises for needy African pastors (i.e. chicken coops!), as well as taking part in medical missions among the Maasai people with Sister Freda.

I just had a large tattoo of an African village put on my back. OK, OK, so some of you don't like tattoos. But it's my way of letting everyone know how I feel about the importance of what God and Sister Freda are doing in Kenya.

COFFEE COMES TO THE FARM

One day in 2004 Sister Freda was in the U.S. visiting in the home of Pastor Chuck and Sue Wells in Crestline, California. In the course of their dinner conversation, Chuck turned to her and said,

"Freda, I notice that you do not grow coffee on your farm. Are you aware that here in the U.S., Kenyan coffee is one of the most expensive and desired coffees sold? If you could grow coffee and we could bring it to the States, we could sell it to folks in the church and send you all of the profits."

That conversation was not forgotten by Sister Freda. Not long after she had returned to Kenya, Chuck received an email: "Pastor Chuck, I have just bought 1000 coffee seedlings." Chuck felt panic setting in, for he knew nothing about growing coffee, the agricultural and import laws that had to be followed, or even how to roast coffee beans.

"How long before the plants will begin to produce coffee, Sister Freda?" Chuck asked.

"About three years," was the answer.

"Phew!" thought Chuck, relieved. "I have a little time to work this out."

The next thing Chuck heard, there were 2,300 coffee plants! This was a big-time project.

Bottom line: the coffee plants have now matured and are bearing fruit. Chuck is now marketing Kenyan coffee which not only brings in income for the ministry but spreads the word about the Medical Center and its broader ministry.

Chuck once asked Sister Freda, "What does it cost to treat a case of malaria?" She told him that for the mild cases it is as little as fifty cents. Even severe cases can be treated for $100. Think what a few pounds of coffee will be able to accomplish![9]

3 THE CRISIS OF ILLITERACY

Promoting and furthering kids' education is a great desire of Sister Freda, for she knows that education is a prime key to breaking the cycle of poverty. Even when tuition is free many parents cannot pay for the uniforms required for their children to attend public school. Furthermore, in many schools the children have no desks or chairs, and must provide their own or sit on a dirt floor. Consequently, many poor children are excluded from schooling and grow up unable to read and write.

In the year 2000 Sister Freda felt compelled to start first a feeding program, and then a school on her compound, in this way reaching the nearby slum children ages three to seven who would otherwise be unable to attend school.

The whole concept developed when mothers brought their sick children to the outpatient clinic, and Sister Freda gave them medicine for their children with instructions that it was to be taken three times a day *with food*. Although she provided the meds without charge, she discovered the mothers were not giving the much-needed medicine to the children. When she investigated, she found that the mothers had no food in their homes to give their children to eat, with or without medicine. Families in these slum villages consider themselves "lucky" to get one meal a day, and many, including the children, go more than a day without a single bite of food.

Because of the constant need in these villages for enough food to stay alive, the parents are generally gone from the home in the daytime, looking for work or something to eat. The children are left in the care of a neighbor or to fend for themselves, with the oldest child caring for the younger ones. Sometimes the "oldest" are too young to be able to hold their baby sisters or brothers on their laps, and can merely rest the babies' heads on their knees to comfort them.

Distressed by this appalling situation, Sister Freda and her husband began a feeding program, starting with thirty-five children. To this day the young kids come to her compound, walking as far as two or three miles to receive porridge mid-morning and a meal in the early afternoon before going home. In addition, on Saturdays they come to receive small parcels of maize and beans. Without those, they would have empty stomachs on Sundays.

When the children began coming to the feeding program, Richard and Sister Freda noticed that they were restless and bored. Government schools were too far away for them to attend even if they could afford to go, and Richard especially became concerned about their education. Sister Freda urged caution before they jumped into adding a school to their already strained budget and energies, but, in his charming British way, Richard said, "Let's do it straight away!"

Presently, about one hundred and twenty-five children are enrolled. The staff includes three teachers (each paid 4,000 shillings, or $60, per month) and two girls who care for five abandoned children (each paid 3,000 shillings, or $45, per month). The children learn to read and write, and they study

English, math, environment, Bible, and health. When they are accepted in Grade One, they are generally the best students in their class — advanced beyond those who have attended the usual kindergarten.

While education is not Sister Freda's primary focus, she has not forgotten the difference schooling made in her life, liberating her from a hand-to-mouth existence to a life of purposeful significance. Her heart reaches out to give that same opportunity to children whose future is hopeless unless they can go to school.

4 THE CRISIS OF SPIRITUAL DARKNESS

Kenya has many, many churches — in fact, officials report 4000 registered congregations[10] and no one knows how many unregistered places of worship exist as well. Still, thousands of small villages do not have a single church. Of course, having a church building in a town is no guarantee that lives are being affected by its presence. Sadly, the church and God are sometimes rejected by the poor because the churches have not demonstrated how God relates to their great needs.

"The churches lack concrete and tangible strategies to combat the tremendous problems the people face," Sister Freda observes. Personally, she has discovered that extending a helping hand to the needy is a powerful way of showing the love of God and opening hearts to the Gospel, which she calls "their #1 need."

When Sister Freda conducts a mobile clinic, she always brings a pastor with her to share the Gospel with the people. Every week Ezekiel Kisaka, pastor of Emmanuel Worship Center, comes to encourage the staff on the Medical Center compound and to pray with each patient, with other pastors coming to minister from time to time as well.

When I asked Sister Freda how the Gospel message is communicated to the patients when they come to the hospital, she explained that in the admissions process, they are asked about their religion. Most people answer either "I am a Christian" or "I don't go to any church." After admission, when Sister Freda prays with each patient, she reads Scripture to them. Then, starting with the Psalms and the Book of John, she teaches them how to read the Bible in such a way that they can understand the meaning for themselves.

When I further inquired as to whether some of them come to faith in Christ during this crisis period of their lives, she answered with a look that told me more than her words: "Oh, yes, entire families become believers" — a natural, expected result of their recognizing their need for spiritual help.

If anyone asks for a Bible, Sister Freda will find some way to get one for the person. About every five or six years Gideons International furnishes a Bible for each bed, and Sister Freda is happy when she finds that patients have taken them home with them.

To Sister Freda's great delight, the local Christian FM radio station, Radio Imani, now furnishes pre-tuned transistor radios for the hospital rooms. This means that the patients can listen to Christian programming all day during their hospital confinement.

Sister Freda has found that responding to a person's medical crisis with compassion and understanding often opens the person's heart to hear the Gospel. What started as a medical need results in an encounter with Jesus Christ that changes someone's eternal destiny.

chapter 10

SISTER FREDA AND
STEVE RUTENBAR

The year was 1996. A 17-year-old Pokot girl lay seriously ill with malaria and meningitis, paralyzed on her left side, and she could not speak. Deb Snell, a missionary with International Christian Ministries, knew that without medical care, Lillian Lolian had no hope. It was a 24-hour drive from near the Uganda border where Deb was located, to Sister Freda's Medical Center — a trip the girl would probably not survive: twenty-four long hours of being bounced, and bumped, and jolted over potholes so deep that the roads were barely drivable. So Deb paid the cost for her to be airlifted to Sister Freda's hospital.

Lillian remained in the hospital for seven long months of treatment, but eventually she recovered and was taken back home. Her hospital bill: nearly 100,000 Kenya shillings — more than $1,500 US today — not a huge amount to some who read these pages, but an enormous amount for someone who has no possible way to earn more than a few dollars a month. Yet Lillian was allowed to leave the hospital with her bill unpaid. If she had been treated at any private health facility in Kenya, she would have been detained until the bill was paid. Sister Freda covered Lillian's medical expenses from her own money.

Appreciating Sister Freda's special care for Lillian, Deb introduced Sister Freda to Pastor Steve Rutenbar in 1997 when he was in Kitale with an outreach team from Saddleback Church. Seeing the vast needs and seeing what Sister Freda was doing to help meet those needs, Pastor Steve prayed with her, and promised, "We'll be back." He kept that promise, and since that first trip he and his outreach teams have been instrumental in enabling hundreds of people from many different churches to visit Sister Freda and channel help to her.

When the people who come with Pastor Steve have seen the needs, they have responded with support in the way of finances, medicines, mosquito nets, clothing, and medical supplies. Teams have helped construct X-ray and dentistry departments at the hospital, provided a well and a generator to operate it, established a micro-enterprise chicken project, and purchased livestock for the farm. Donors have added a wing to the hospital, providing more examining rooms, office space, and another room for surgery.

Sister Freda says, "At times I've accumulated huge debts at the local pharmacies. We've prayed, and visiting groups have settled the bill for me. In addition, they have provided food for needy orphans, widows, destitutes, and children."

A missionary's compassionate concern for a 17-year-old girl and a Kenyan nurse's sacrificial care for the girl, who could do nothing to repay her, resulted in an American's visit for ministry that led to many, many people having their eyes opened to and hearts touched by the needs of Kenya — people not only from Saddleback Church but from numerous other churches as well. Happenstance? I don't think so.

chapter 11

INSPIRING OTHERS TO GET INVOLVED

Deep in the trenches of poverty, disease and despair, Sister Freda carries with her the sweet fragrance of Christ, a fragrance that refreshes not only those she serves but also those who look on. Numerous outreaches have been established because her infectious concern has inspired people to get involved. Lydia Monroe, founder of Oasis of Hope, a ministry to the street children of Kitale, says Sister Freda showed her that a person doesn't have to be some saintly, extraordinary, other-worldly type to do something for God. "You don't have to start out special," says Lydia, "you just have to start."

Consider, for instance, Marjaana's story . . . .

TAKE THE FIRST STEP
by Marjaana

As a child in my native Finland, I always wanted to be a missionary in Africa. But Africa is a long ways from Finland. The chance seemed so remote that I would ever even visit the continent. But God used Sister Freda in my life to make it happen.

By the time I met her I was living in California and attending Saddleback Valley Community Church. She was introduced to the congregation at a Sunday service that focused on global missions.

When Sister Freda urged the people, "Come to Africa!" my heart was pounding, "I'm going! I'm going!" In fact, I was one of the first to sign up for the next trip — I was compelled to go.

Once in Kenya, we were organized in small groups to visit a variety of churches. My group was taken to a small congregation that met in a metal shack at the back of the market in Kiminini. The church had a dirt floor and the people were very poor. But I felt the Spirit of God when the pastor, Shadrack Barasa, was sharing. He had started a polytechnic school in the church to teach mechanics, carpentry and sewing. He had only two sewing machines for the 200 people who wanted to learn!

I was disturbed. He was doing so much with so little. I asked myself, "What am I doing with the resources I have in Orange County, California? Nothing!"

Back at home, I was determined — yes, even driven — to return to Kenya, this time with the other five (scared!) members of my ladies' small group. Preparing for the trip, I contacted Pastor Shadrack and asked him, "What would you like us to do?"

His response: "Why don't you bring a medical team with you and do a clinic?" He later added a request for a Women's Conference in response to my modest wish to meet with the women of his church.

Our group had absolutely no medical experience and none of us was a public speaker — unlikely prospects. But after I prayed, I felt peace replace panic.

I knew we had to have three things in order to operate the clinic: staff, supplies, and medicines. I contacted Sister Freda, who wrote back to me, "Don't worry about the staff. I'll have all the doctors and nurses and pharmacists you'll need — free of charge."

At a party in California I sat next to a nurse I didn't know — Eithne Keegan (*see* Chapter 3), and I shared the needs with her. Eithne assured me,

"Don't worry. I have connections." In a few weeks my garage was crammed full of medical supplies.

I decided to make it hard for God by setting a goal of raising $10,000 for meds so I would be assured this was God's plan, not just ours. When the time came to go, we had raised $10,000 for meds and $4000 for the conference!

I had told Sister Freda that we had a good amount of money for the medicines. Later she told me she thought perhaps we would have between $1000 and $2000 U.S. When we gathered in Sister Freda's yard, I made the presentation to her. "I have $10,000 in an envelope for you," I announced. She literally sank to the ground and wept tears of joy. She couldn't speak. Together we went to town to buy meds for the clinic and her hospital. I was overjoyed when the pharmacist sold them to us at his cost.

More than 3000 people were treated over the two-day period of the clinic held at Pastor Shadrack's church. Sister Freda herself was there helping us. We showed the Jesus Film in the church for people to watch while they waited to be treated, and more than 100 accepted Christ!

I don't have space to tell about the Women's Conference, but as a result of our time there, the six women that made up our group have established a ministry called Ordinary Women, believing God uses ordinary people to do extraordinary things. We have been able to drill wells for water, organize citywide crusades, and now are helping the local pastors work together to find their own solution to the plight of orphans in their area. While Ordinary Women helps raise funds, the Kenyan churches take ownership of the program.

None of this would have happened if Sister Freda's heart had not overflowed into our lives.

chapter 12

How Does She Do It?

Whenever we encounter people who have accomplished much in life, who have truly achieved significance, we naturally wonder, "What's the secret? How do they do it?" These are fair questions to ask Sister Freda, and the answers reveal not only the strength that equips this African woman but provide powerful insights for us as well.

Four internal resources enable Sister Freda to do what she does:

First and foremost, she prays. When Sister Freda's humanity reaches its limits, she pours her heart out to God, the One to whom she can vent her problems. Many times at a point of desperate need, she has found relief by falling back on God's promise,

> Cast your cares on the Lord and he will sustain
> you; he will never let the righteous fall.
>
> Psalm 55:22

As she so often says, "We pray because God answers our prayers!"

Second, Sister Freda has a tenacious faith in God's provision, for He has proven His faithfulness to her in countless situations. She knows Whom she believes in and has placed her trust in time and time again. "God will take care of you if you follow Him," she explains simply.

A third and vital driving force that moves Sister Freda is that she knows her calling. She is unremittingly motivated by one of her favorite Bible verses, "Each one should use whatever gift he has received to serve others, faithfully administering God's grace in its various forms" (1 Peter 4:10). When she feels overwhelmed by the immensity of her responsibility, she recognizes that God has gifted her so she can serve others. This motivates her renewed obedience to God's mission for her life.

"Sister Freda has a remarkable ability to remain calm in the middle of whatever is going on around her," notes volunteer David Storm. "I have never seen her panic. She is not in a rush, yet she gets everything done. I have observed her with 300 people lined up at her clinic waiting to be seen, yet she remains patient and loving."

Sister Freda's peace in the middle of emergencies is a direct result of her "purpose-driven life," the outcome of knowing that she is doing exactly what God designed her to do.

In charge of a multi-faceted ministry that would overwhelm most people, Sister Freda nonetheless has a humble heart to do the servant's task.

SHE LIVES TO SERVE
by Michele

When my husband and I visit Sister Freda and her husband, Richard, we always walk the farm with Richard, for he means a lot to me — the grandpa I never had. The last time I was there, it had been raining, and by the time we got back to the little house on the compound from our walk, my shoes were covered with mud, and my socks were wet.

Sister Freda came running across the grass from the hospital just as we arrived at the cottage. She insisted that I sit down and let her take off my muddy shoes so that she could clean them. I objected strongly, not wanting this very special lady to do such a lowly task.

"No, Sister Freda, you don't have to do that. I can clean them myself."

When I refused, she knelt down and took my foot and began taking off my shoe even while I was standing. I was forced to sit down at that point in order to maintain my balance. Sister Freda does not take no for an answer! I looked at Richard and half-seriously and half-jokingly said,

"Richard, can you please stop your wife?"

"It's no use, Michele," said Richard. "I've tried before, and it doesn't work. Freda can be quite persistent."

A short time later, Sister Freda returned with the clean shoes — and a cup of tea and refreshments.

Spiritual discernment is the fourth resource that enables Sister Freda to know how best to meet the needs of others. Guided by God's gentle promptings, she is able to discern both physical and emotional needs of those the Lord brings to her or lays on her heart, and quickly responds to meet their needs.

It was 2 a.m. in California, when Pastor Steve was roused from sleep by the ringing phone.

"Hello."

"It's Sister Freda. Pastor Steve, are you OK?"

While she had been praying in Kenya, God had showed Sister Freda that something was wrong with Steve. She called immediately and learned that he was scheduled for surgery the next morning.

"Sister Freda surely has the gift of discernment," says Lisa Romesburg, organizer for Pastor Steve's trips. "She immediately knows your heart. A highly intuitive person, she knows if you are hurting or in pain. She often lays her hand on someone and assures him or her, 'God knows your pain.'"

Her discernment leads her to recognize the needs of the heart as well as the body. She knows the importance of touch. If you are ill, she will caringly hold your hand or softly touch your shoulder, for well she knows that this can be every bit as important as medicine for healing. Yet, when you are with her, you realize her touch is not merely a "bedside manner" but her responsive impulse, the overflow of a heart of compassion.

Sustained and spurred on by these four — prayer, faith, obedience to God's command to use her gifts, and with loving spiritual discernment of people's needs — Sister Freda draws resources God provides to minister faithfully to both body and spirit.

chapter 13

FOREVER GRATEFUL

What joy there will be in heaven someday when we hear a stream of Kenyans testify, "My life was saved and my future transformed because of Sister Freda." Her compassionate heart and caring hands have changed life for Anne and Catherine, for Councilor Sawenja, and for a young Kitale man who worked in a dairy — and they will forever be grateful. Their stories give us glimpses of Sister Freda at work.

■ Anne Omare dropped by Sister Freda's house one morning while I was visiting just to say hello to her. As Sister Freda went about the house taking care of various matters, giving Anne and me time to chat and enjoy getting acquainted, I learned in the course of our conversation that several years before Anne was born, her mother had been at the point of death with an ectopic pregnancy. Her mother had bled so much that she would not survive surgery unless she could receive a transfusion. But Sister Freda had no blood supply at the hospital. The woman's blood type was A-positive — almost miraculously the same type as both Sister Freda's and the surgeon's. The two of them — Sister Freda and the surgeon — each gave a pint of blood and then proceeded with the surgery. Not only was her life saved, but later she became pregnant again — with Anne.

Anne told me she was one of thirty-four children (seven of them borne by her own mother). Her father had three wives and all of the wives lived together in one house. At first I wondered if I had heard her correctly.

"You must have many cousins," I commented.

"About a year ago there were ninety-five," Anne responded, "but by now there are probably close to two hundred."

Then she shared about the time when her brother was in a coma for two weeks. They took him to Sister Freda's hospital, and although the family could not afford to pay much, Sister Freda did not turn him away but nursed him back to health. Anne says, "If they had taken him to another hospital in such condition, he would certainly have been set aside to die." It is no surprise that Anne loves Sister Freda and says she is a very special inspiration to their family.

One morning Sister Freda took me on a tour of the slum villages surrounding her medical center. Everywhere we went people waved and greeted her.

"I've treated just about everyone around here," commented the "reluctant celebrity" to me as we bounced along the rutted roads. It was a beautiful morning, but we pressed on quickly so that she could introduce me to the many people she wanted me to meet before the afternoon rains turned the roads into red rivers of mud.

We stopped to meet a woman who lives in a one-room mud-and-sticks house just like the one Sister Freda grew up in. In one corner was the open fireplace. Another corner had space for a baby calf to spend the night in safety. In a third corner the children would sleep on the dirt floor, with their parents sleeping in the fourth corner. There was not a piece of furniture in the house.

Most of the people in this area rent a tiny corner on someone's farm where they can put up a bare-bones home. The neighborhoods are filled with smiling children who know Sister Freda as the kind person who loves them and helps make them well. It is from these areas that the young children come to Sister Freda's feeding program and preschool.

■ Visiting Catherine and her baby, Isaac, was a touching experience.

Catherine's husband died of AIDS in 2003, and now Catherine lives with the disease herself. But because of Sister Freda's intervention during Catherine's pregnancy, little Isaac has been spared and is a beautiful baby, healthy and strong.

Knowing that he was going to die and leave her a widow, Catherine's husband built her a small but comfortable house. But the sad fact is that outside her home are two mounds — one is the grave of her husband and the other marks the spot where another child is buried.

With the vitamins that Sister Freda gives her and coaching in good nutrition, Catherine has a very good chance of seeing her little boy grow up. I could see the joy expressed in her warm smiles and her delight in seeing Sister Freda. She asked me to take a picture of her and her son and send it to her — probably the only one she will ever have in her possession.

- A man who is an area councilor (an elected position) was brought in to Sister Freda's Medical Center with what Kenyans call "acute abdomen." Councilor Sawenja was an acquaintance of Freda's, and he desperately needed emergency surgery. But the doctor refused.

"He has a bad infection of the colon and also adhesions. His condition is inoperable," the doctor told Freda.

"Surely you can help him," Freda responded. "He has so many children, and his wife is pregnant."

The doctor bristled. "Do you know how long it will take to go in there and clean up that mess? It's going to take more than four hours, and we may run out of oxygen."

But when she feels strongly about an issue, the Gentle Nurse resolutely stands her ground. "We will do suchand-such," she will say quietly but with a firmness that defies argument. On this occasion Sister Freda hung on.

"Let's try," she urged. The doctor and nurse began the surgery, cleaning out the infection, injecting antibiotics as they proceeded. Out went the dead portion of intestine and the ends were rejoined. Three successful hours later the man was wheeled back to the ward to recover. That was about twenty years ago.

■ A 22-year-old young man was working in a milk plant in Kitale, when something went wrong with the pasteurizing equipment he was using. Without warning, and seemingly in an instant, he found himself severely burned from his neck to his knees by blistering steam. One can only imagine the pain he experienced.

He was brought to the hospital, and Sister Freda began not only to treat him but to pray for him.

"He's going to get well," she said assuredly, confident that God heard her. The terrible burns healed amazingly in a record-breaking three weeks.

These four are just a few representatives of the many Kenyans who will be forever grateful that God called Sister Freda to serve the needy — and she answered His call.

chapter 14

THE FACILITATOR

There is no limit to what can be accomplished
if it doesn't matter who gets the credit.[1]
Ralph Waldo Emerson

Some gifted leaders have a sort of "tunnel vision" when it comes to the importance of accomplishing their own goals, and, therefore, are disinclined to help with other people's projects. Not Sister Freda. She is just as eager to help *others* accomplish their goals, to assist *others* in their projects, to translate for *others* who don't speak Swahili, or to provide medical personnel for *others* who want to conduct clinics as she is to see her "own" goals accomplished. She seemingly has no concern about who receives the credit. What she *is* concerned about is that her people are helped.

Her heart breaks when she sees a child who is mistreated or neglected, and if no one else will help, she will care for that child herself. So, her joy knows no bounds when someone else takes on the responsibility to see needy children cared for in a loving environment. Sister Freda will do all in her power to help those who want to sponsor a child, enabling a life-changing transformation. Never was that more true than in the case of Derek and Reggie.

THE STORY OF DEREK AND REGGIE

Dan and Kathleen Hamer first encountered Kenya when their son Philip, age 19, went there with ten college men on a Christian ministry trip with Pastor Steve. Philip was enrolled in film school at the time, and when he returned to the U.S. he presented his short documentary as a school assignment for Chapman University Film School — about John, a boy at Tumaini Home who had been orphaned by AIDS. He called it, simply, "John's Story."[2]

When the Hamers saw the film, their hearts were broken. "It's one thing to know the fact that kids are dying of AIDS in Africa. It's another thing to sit and look at a film your own son has made of what is happening," the Hamers explained.

Growing up in a pastor's family, Kathleen had always been afraid God would send her as a missionary to Africa. Her prayer was always "Anywhere but Africa, Lord." Pastor Steve kept telling the Hamers stories about Kenya, but Kathleen was deathly afraid of flying and, in fact, hadn't flown in five years. Besides, she had health issues that contributed to her fears.

Then in March of 2003 Pastor Steve brought Sister Freda to the U.S. — and to the Hamers' home to pray for their daughter, Erica, who had serious health problems. Sister Freda laid hands on Erica and prayed a remarkable prayer for her healing.

Then she said to her, "You will come to Africa," a seeming impossibility with Erica's health condition.

Almost abruptly Sister Freda then turned to Kathleen and said, "I need to pray for you, too." Sister Freda had not been told that Kathleen has an autoimmune system problem similar to lupus that gives her terrible headaches and other symptoms. Sister Freda put her hands on Kathleen's head and began to pray. Kathleen felt the power of God coming into her body through Sister Freda's hands as she prayed. Not only did Sister Freda pray about her headaches but she also prayed,

"This mama has a lot of fears. Jesus, release her from her fears." Kathleen's heart was melted by the prayer. Sister Freda knew nothing about the fears locked deep in Kathleen's heart. Then Sister Freda looked her in the eyes and said,

"And you will come to Africa, too."

From this point on, healing began in Kathleen's body and continued over a period of time. Now Kathleen's prayer was, "Lord, if I'm going to Africa, you'll have to make me able to go." Her Bible verse for the trip was Philippians 1:21: "For to me, to live is Christ and to die is gain" — perhaps not a very comforting verse for the rest of the group on the plane! She was pretty sure she was going to die.

Years before this, Kathleen and Dan had longed for another child and considered international adoption. But health problems in their family made it unwise for them to follow through. As they left on the plane for Kenya with Philip and Patrick, their two sons, Erica — who had to stay behind because of her health — teasingly pleaded, "Mama, bring me home a baby!"

IN KENYA

While the Hamers were in Kitale they questioned Sister Freda about the feasibility of adopting a child in Kenya but then the topic was dropped. Both sons thought it would be great to adopt a Kenyan child, but Dan disagreed: "It *wouldn't* be great. We're too old," etc., etc. Then on their tenth day there, they met Derek.

Now the story turns, as we observe God's hand of guidance in the lives of another couple: John and Sandi West, who were on that same ministry-trip with the Hamers.

The day in Kitale, when John met Derek, touched his heart as no other, he says. The group visited Deliverance Church, not far from Sister Freda's Medical Center, where they took part in the church's weekly street kids' washing and feeding program. About eight hundred kids were there, waiting for a bath and a meal. Pastor Steve asked for one of the kids to volunteer so he could show the Americans how to bathe the little ones. A Kitale lad named Derek, who looked to be about four years old, readily volunteered to strip and let Steve wash him. As John watched them, Steve turned to Dan Hamer, "Would you help me bathe him?" Afterwards he handed Derek to Dan's wife, Kathleen, to dry him off. Derek was shivering, and she had no towel.

"He's cold and wet, Steve, and I don't have anything to dry him with."

"Kathleen, I've got eight hundred kids waiting to be bathed. Just put his clothes back on," Steve insisted. Holding Derek close to keep him warm, Kathleen felt a maternal instinct for him begin to grow in her heart.

All that afternoon Derek was tugging either on Steve's hand — or John's or Dan's or Patrick's. He just wouldn't leave them alone. John said he felt the Spirit of God "oozing" out of little Derek — even though Derek didn't know much about God at that time. Then John's male "fix-it" approach kicked in — or was it an idea from God? He turned to Steve, "Maybe we could get Derek into Tumaini Orphanage."

"We don't know for sure, John, that he is actually an orphan," Steve responded. "Maybe he has a family somewhere. We need to find out." Soon Sister Freda, Steve, and Philip were on their way to Derek's home — three adults led by a five-year-old!

"Turn here, now turn there," . . . for five miles.

When they arrived at the place where Derek lived, they met a woman who said she was Derek's grandmother. Sister Freda and Steve explained why they were there. Overjoyed, Derek's grandmother exclaimed, "I've been praying for angels to come and take him away!" (Derek's mother was on drugs and not in the home.) Steve and Sister Freda also noticed another little boy there, seemingly about two years old, who turned out to be Derek's brother, Reggie.[3] The grandmother told them to go ahead and take Derek and put him in the orphanage, but Derek's little brother was too young to be admitted.

That evening Steve walked into the dining hall of the Kitale Club with Derek on his shoulders. Everyone cheered, thrilled that a little boy's life and future was going to be saved. When Derek was put down from Steve's shoulders, he made a bee-line straight for Dan, crawling under the tables to reach Dan's lap. Kathleen was sitting directly across from her husband, and in that moment she heard God speak to her audibly, "This is your son — take him home."

"I think we need to adopt him, Mom," said Patrick. "I heard God too."

And how did Dan respond? "We'll adopt *this one*."

"Are you serious?" Kathleen asked.

"Kathleen, I heard God say we're supposed to adopt him."

But there's more to the story. A couple of days before the Hamers met Derek, they had received word that their daughter, Erica, who was back in California, was in the emergency room with a severe heart problem. Can you imagine how Kathleen felt standing under a banana tree in Kitale, talking on the cell phone with an emergency room doctor 9,500 miles away?

Erica recovered, but Kathleen made arrangements to call her the next day to be sure she was all right. Of course, at this time Erica knew absolutely nothing about Derek. When Kathleen called and was assured that Erica was okay, before she could tell her she was going to have a little brother, Erica blurted,

"Mom, I had the craziest dream. I dreamed you got off the plane with a little African boy, named Derek!"

Stranger yet was the fact that at this point, the Hamers, who had asked Derek his name, thought he said his name was *Eric*. When Kathleen heard about Erica's dream, she thought, "Oh, well, 'Eric' is close enough to 'Derek.'" Shortly, they were to learn, however, that they had misunderstood this little boy: his name was, indeed, *Derek*.

Sister Freda checked Derek medically and discovered he had three-foot-long worms, malaria and fever. John said, "If Derek has these things wrong with him, Reggie must as well." Hamers had made the decision to adopt Derek, but Reggie couldn't be left behind.

ADOPTION

Now began the tedious adoption process for the two boys. Although Kenya does not allow foreigners easily to adopt their children, the Hamers finally located a woman attorney in Nairobi who would help them, and had her begin work on the adoption.

The Hamers returned home and completed everything they could possibly do to adopt Derek and Reggie. Then in July 2004 Dan and Philip flew to Nairobi for an appointment with the attorney. There they received the heart-rending news, "I'm sorry, but you can't adopt Derek. There is just no way." Dejected beyond words, they said, "Well, at least we can go to Kitale and see him before we go home."

Upon their arrival, they were greeted by Sister Freda and Rev. Stephen Mairori, head of ICM Ministries in Kenya.

"We know an attorney and a judge who might be able to help. Let's go talk to them," was their encouraging greeting.

Downtown they went to the new attorney's office — Sister Freda, Stephen Mairori, Dan, Philip, Derek and Reggie. The next stop was court, where they waited for seven long hours. But the judge would not hear their case. The court was in recess for the next two weeks, so nothing was left to do but go to the court in Kisumu (a three-and-a-half hour drive) the next day. Added to the entourage at this time were the boys' grandmother and their previously missing birth mother, who had abandoned the boys shortly after giving birth. Surprisingly, the judge wanted to meet with only two of the group: Sister Freda and Rev. Mairori. In closed session the judge asked them,

"Do you think this adoption is best for the children?"

Sister Freda and Stephen assured them that it was. For the past nearly two years Derek had been basically living on the street. He knew what it was to be beaten, kicked and abused. And he knew hunger. His stomach crying for a morsel to eat, Derek would walk five miles to scrounge for food in a garbage dump. A man who ran a restaurant sometimes took pity on him and gave him scraps of food. He would eat half and then walk five miles back to the village to bring the other half home to Reggie. On at least one occasion, Reggie was put in a trash barrel "so he wouldn't get lost" and, of course, munched on the garbage he found there.

The boys desperately needed a stable home.

"Then the Hamers may have them," the judge declared. In exactly four days the boys were theirs.

As is fairly common in Kenya, the boys had no birth certificates. Though everyone usually has a tribal ID, this mother did not have even that. But Sister Freda was not one to be stopped by government red tape. "They *will* have birth certificates," she declared. And under God's hand, eventually, the official birth certificates were produced by the government office.

On August 28, 2004, Derek and Reggie arrived in America. Derek was six then, and Reggie was three, although the boys' exact birthdates are unknown. When Dan and Philip got off the plane with the boys, Reggie, who had never seen Kathleen before, came running to her with open arms, "Mama, how are you? How are you?" he called out.

Because of the prevalence of AIDS in Kenya, with some 30 percent of Kenya's children affected, the boys had to be tested several times. When they visited the doctor in California, he noticed a distinct T-shaped scar on the inside of Reggie's wrist.

"I know what that is," the doctor said. "That scar comes only from having a full body blood exchange."

"Yes, they put the blood in there," interrupted his brother, Derek. Then he was able to explain that before Reggie was two years old, he had become deathly ill. "I was watching him die," he said. "Then a pastor came — I'd never seen him before — and took Reggie to the district hospital."

The California doctor said that Reggie had probably had cerebral malaria, deadliest of all malaria strains, a full body blood exchange being one of the primary treatments for this kind of malaria. It is remarkable that the pastor "happened" to take Reggie to a hospital big enough to be able to carry out this life-saving procedure — a local clinic could not have done it. The blood had likely come from the World Blood Bank, for it was free of AIDS. Derek said they never saw the pastor again. No one in the neighborhood knew who he was. An angel, perhaps?

As a result, two little Kenyan boys who had no hope of a future are now being raised by godly parents in Foothill Ranch,

California. The Hamers will never doubt that God intends for Reggie and Derek to be in their family.

After the boys had been in the States awhile (the boys learned English in three months), their sister, Erica, asked Derek, "How did you end up at Deliverance Church that day?"

"Very sick," Derek responded. "Tummy hurt. So I asked my friend, 'What should I do?'"

"You should pray to God," his friend responded.

"I prayed, and God said, 'Go to Deliverance Church.' And," added Derek, quite decisively, "that's how I met my mother!"

The Hamers' companion in short-term missions, John West, believes God used him to ask the question of Pastor Steve, "Can we get him in Tumaini?" Otherwise Derek and Reggie would still be in Kenya. Kathleen agrees. "If God hadn't prompted John to ask the question, we wouldn't have these two precious boys."

"And if it hadn't been for Sister Freda we could never have completed the adoption."

I'm not sure who experienced the most joy — the Hamers, because their long-awaited desire to adopt children was fulfilled, or Sister Freda, because two children, who would probably not have survived, now have a loving home and a bright future.

And, Sister Freda's prayer for Erica was answered in August 2006, when Erica was able to join a ministry team and come to Kenya, just as Sister Freda had predicted.

chapter 15

ON-GOING STORY. . .

As I was beginning to do research for this book, some printed material was given to me about Sister Freda, and one sentence near the end caught my attention. "In addition, she [Sister Freda] wants to see a Nurses' Training Center established on the property to ensure that there will always be a staff to allow the hospital to continue its outreach."

Great idea! Many of the young women of Kitale would like to become nurses but they cannot afford to go to Nairobi for training. A nursing school right there on the hospital property would allow them to receive the education they need. The Medical Center would, in turn, benefit because there would always be staff available.

A short time after I read this, I was talking to John West about his time in Kitale. Following his first visit, John's desire to help Sister Freda had prompted him to help her complete the second wing of the Medical Center. He mentioned to me that there was one more thing he would like to see built: a nurses' training school so that Sister Freda's work could continue indefinitely. "I think God wants me to help her do this," John added.

"Yes," I said. "She says this is a project she wants very badly. Listen to this, John. In her last letter to me, she asked me to pray that she can complete 'the nurses' home whose foundation we started three years ago.'" I presumed that Sister Freda and John had been talking together about plans for the center.

John looked at me incredulously, and for a moment he said nothing. "Darlene, I've never talked to her about this. I just felt God wanted me to help build a nurses' training center."

"You haven't discussed this with her, John?"

"No!" he assured me. And then we both had that tingling sensation that God was at work.

God had done it again! As He does so often when He wants something accomplished, God planted a vision for the work in one heart and the desire to enable the work in the heart of another. As this book is being written, the building is being erected for a nursing academy. And Sister Freda says the first three students will be three girls from Tumaini Orphanage who were rescued from life on the streets. Now doesn't that sound like something Sister Freda would do!

Sister Freda is a firm believer in the combination of prayer and hard work. To quote her, "We can do all things through Christ, who strengthens us!" And my conviction is that her vision will never diminish so long as there is a needy person crying out for help.

chapter 16

"TELL THEM TO COME"

> A life devoted to material comforts and thrills is like throwing money down a rathole. But a life invested in the labor of love yields dividends of pure joy unsurpassed and unending.
>
> John Piper[1]

"If you had to live your life over again, what would you do differently?" I asked Sister Freda.

Almost facetiously, she responded with a smile, "Send everybody to school, and build more churches and schools — and build roads." But then she continued, thoughtfully,

> Personally, I am happy with life as it is. I don't want to live it over. I'm very happy with who I am and what I'm doing. With Paul, "I consider my life worth nothing to me, if only I may finish the race and complete the task the Lord Jesus has given me," Acts 20:24.

Lunch was finished, but we lingered at the table reminiscing together about the path along which God had led her in the past and talking about what she still wants to accomplish in the future — the laps of the race yet to be finished.

So long as people around her are suffering, children are hungry, and the poor face a bleak future, Sister Freda will want to do more. She especially wants to see the nursing academy completed and functioning — a big project which will need assistance.

Those who come to visit Sister Freda and to help in her work see that she is always trying to do more to change the lives of people who live in hopelessness. If she has a fault, it is "spreading herself too thin" as she continues to see people in need she would like to help.

Yet Sister Freda has a big welcome mat out for those who would come to see her ministry. As we reluctantly ended our time together, her closing words to me were spoken with urgency, "Tell the people to come and visit me. Yes, tell them to come. Come meet the children whose stories are in this book. Meet Esther — meet Moses — meet Morgan, Davis and Lucy. Tell them to come!"

chapter 17

BUILDING A BRIDGE

Even though the world is fast becoming a global village, in which you can travel from Los Angeles to Nairobi in just seventeen hours, the cultural distance between Africa and the West is still great. For instance, Kenya, has a well-educated elite who are at home in any upper-class environment in their own country or abroad. Yet there are still many in this developing country who have not had the advantage of education that would help them develop an accurate world view. For them the gap remains wide.

Pastor Chuck Wells was standing near the area at Kitale Deliverance Church where food is cooked for the children in Purpose-Driven Academy. A woman came up to him and asked, "Pastor Chuck, why is it that every time you come here, you fly?" She was, of course, inferring that it costs a lot of money to ride airplanes.

"I can explain that," he assured her. "You see, the reason I fly is that I live in California, and it's a very long distance from California to Kenya."

"You could drive."

Chuck realized he had some further explaining to do. "Well, the problem with driving is that there is a very big ocean between California and Africa."

With confidence, she quickly responded, "But you Americans — you could build a bridge!"

Yes, Africans do look to the West for help to build that bridge. And in a sense, that is what this book attempts to do: to build a bridge of communication and understanding about Kenya's needs and one amazing woman's efforts to help meet those needs.

Sister Freda has built bridges to the poor, the ill, the uneducated, and the downtrodden. Let me assure you that Sister Freda would be the first to tell you she is not the only one working to help the needy in Kitale. There's Margaret and Moses, and Patricia, and Julius and Jane. And Eliud, and Stephen and Roslyn, and Geoffrey and many, many others — all giving their lives and energies to relieve suffering and change lives.

And there's room for you too. You can reach out to help Freda do what she cannot do alone.

Many people say they don't feel a "call" to missions because they've never heard a voice or seen handwriting on the wall that says, "You should be a missionary!" I like Dr. David Stevens' definition of "the call." He says a call is seeing a need and knowing that you have the ability to do something about it.[1] In that sense, every single one of us is "called." God doesn't expect us to do what we can't do, but He does expect us to do the things we *can* do. He says, "Just look at the field that is white for harvest; use the abilities I have given you, and I will help you."

William Booth, founder of The Salvation Army in London, once said:[2]

> Not called, did you say? Not *heard* the call, I think you should say.
>
> Put your ear down to the Bible and hear Him bid you go and pull sinners out of the fire of sin. Put your ear down to the heart of burdened, agonized humanity and listen to its pitiful wail for help. Go stand by the gates of hell and hear the damned entreat you to go to their father's house and bid their brothers and sisters and servants and masters not to come there.
>
> And then look Christ in the face, whose mercy you have professed to obey, and tell Him whether you will join heart and soul and body and circumstances in the march to publish His mercy to the rest of the world.
>
> That is our call!

Those are powerful words. Every time I read them I'm stirred to ask God if there is more I can do. I hope you are too.

One cannot focus on the life of Sister Freda without quickly recognizing how important is prayer, in all that she accomplishes. But her confidence in prayer arises from something even deeper — the bedrock of her life — and that is her personal relationship with Jesus Christ. Because of Sister Freda's close relationship with Jesus, she sees opportunity and responsibility through His eyes. Because she loves Him, she has offered herself to be His heart and hands and feet for the needy of Kenya.

Ravi Zacharias puts it well:

> Through all the visitations of life — successes or fail-ures — it is not how well you are known or not known. It is not how big your organization is or isn't. It is not even how many sermons one has preached or books one has written or millions of dollars one has accumulated. It is *how well do you know Jesus?* That's it. That is what shapes how you view every-thing else.[3]

May each one of us have a relationship with God that fills our hearts with His compassion, until we touch lives with hands that care.

> Be devoted to one another in brotherly love.
> Honor one another above yourselves.
> Never be lacking in zeal, but keep your spiritual
>   fervor, serving the Lord.
> Be joyful in hope, patient in affliction, faithful in prayer.
> Share with God's people who are in need.
>   Practice hospitality.
>
> Romans 12:10–13

AFTERWORD

· ·

HOW DO YOU HANDLE RESPONSIBILITY
ONCE YOU'VE SEEN GREAT NEED?

My husband had just returned home from ministry overseas. Since the best way to beat jet lag is to spend time in the sun to help a person's internal clock adjust, my husband reasoned, "What better way than to meet a friend for a round of golf?"

At the 9th hole, he picked up a couple of bottles of Snapple — total cost $3. Then reality hit home. A few days ago he had been in a country where $3 is exactly what most pastors receive in a week!

How do we reconcile great need with responsibility? How do you?

These principles can serve as a guide:

REALIZE WHO YOU ARE

   . . . that you cannot right all the wrongs in the world.

   . . . that you are probably not responsible for the cause of the need.

   . . . that it is God, however, who has allowed you to have firsthand knowledge of the need.

   . . . that with knowledge of needs comes some degree of responsibility.

   . . . that you can help *someone*, and for that person you *can* make all the difference in the world.

<u>Understand what you have</u>

- Compare what you have with what the need is — the Bible says to give as God has prospered you.

> On the first day of every week, each one of you should set aside a sum of money in keeping with his income.
>
> 1 Corinthians 16:2

- Bible principle: If you have two coats and your brother has none, you should share.

> The man with two tunics should share with him who has none, and the one who has food should do the same.
>
> Luke 3:11

- Be willing to give, but avoid throwing money at the situation in order to quiet your conscience.
- Don't wait until you're rich to give:

> It's not what you'd do with your money
> if riches should be your lot
> — it's what you're doing right now
> with the dollar and a quarter you've got.

Remember Jesus commended the poor woman who gave two small copper coins, saying, "She did what she could!" God never holds you accountable for what you can't do or where you cannot go, but He does hold you responsible for doing what you can.

RECOGNIZE YOUR PARTNERSHIP WITH GOD

- Pray the Lord of the Harvest to send laborers into HIS harvest.

  Ask the Lord of the harvest, therefore, to send out workers into his harvest field.
  Matthew 9:38

You may not be the one to go, but pray for God's solution.
- Pray about the needs until God tells you what you should do; then be sensitive to the Spirit's voice — and obey.
- God has not given us the burden of understanding poverty, only the obligation to be obedient.

TEN PRACTICAL GUIDELINES
FOR HELPING SISTER FREDA

1   **How is Sister Freda's work supported? Where does she get the money to do this?** Richard and Freda have limited personal funds, yet they give sacrificially of their own money to treat people who cannot pay. Richard's work on the farm is vital to the existence of the Center. But even more vital are the contributions of those whose hearts are also touched with compassion for the needy. The Medical Center operates from day to day on what is available.

2   **What is the biggest need Sister Freda has?** Bluntly, money. She has to buy medicines, corn and beans to feed one hundred and twenty-five kids two meals a day, pay doctors and nurses, buy tea leaves, fuel — the list seems never-ending. In addition, she strives to relieve as much suffering as possible among the displaced persons of Kenya. Money given to her to buy things locally goes much further than when Americans buy goods in the U.S. to send to her, and customs problems are avoided.

   The cost of transporting patients for additional care is ongoing, as well as the costs involved in the nursing academy. Both small gifts and large are highly appreciated.

3   **How can I send money to her?** You can send gifts for Sister Freda to:

> Guidelines Inc.
> Box G
> Laguna Hills, CA 92654
> www.guidelines.org

Indicate that your gift is for the work of Sister Freda. Your contribution is tax-deductible and will be forwarded to her.

4   **I'm in the medical field. Can I really be of help if I'm there only a couple of weeks?** Yes, definitely. Freda has to pay the local doctors and nurses who help at the hospital. Sometimes this involves bringing a specialist from some distance. You may be exactly the help she needs. God often meets Freda's needs this way. Needed are not only doctors and nurses but paramedics, dentists, oral surgeons, optometrists, physician's assistants, and LVNs.

5   **I'm a businessperson. Can I help?** Yes, particularly if you have the talent, experience, patience and willingness to help develop micro-enterprises. Sister Freda is always looking for people with capable management skills as well. You might be surprised how God matches your gifts with Kenya's needs. Ask Sister Freda where she needs help.

6   **Can I send things to help Sister Freda?** The jury is out
concerning whether goods can be shipped to Kenya without involving Sister Freda in having to pay duty to receive
them. Anyone, however, can take commodities to her in
his or her own personal luggage.

7   **What about the medicines I have that I cannot use? Could
they be used by Sister Freda?** Not really. In the past Sister
Freda has been given medicines for which there is little
need in Kenya, as well as out-of-date medications. Far better is to purchase MAP International (Medical Assistance
Program) Travel Packs. $400 buys $10,000 worth of medicines and supplies highly needed in Kenya. Call toll free at
1-800-225-8550. If, however, you have connections with
drug companies and can obtain up-to-date medications,
keep in mind that her needs include antibiotics, pain-
killers, and drugs to treat ulcers, worms, diabetes, high blood
pressure, meningitis and TB. Surgical instruments and
materials would be of great help as well.

8   **Can I go on my own to visit Sister Freda's work in Kitale?**
Sister Freda always wants to open the eyes of people to the
needs and opportunities in Kenya. She yearns to have
people become aware, and she always needs more help.
When I talked to her, over and over she would say, "Please
— tell them to come." In her zeal and generous spirit, she
will say, "Come stay with me." But in actuality, doing that
would be more a burden than a help to her. Find a church

or church group that has a heart for Kenya and come with that group. Or you can find a Christian travel agency that will help you, such as :

> Heather Smith
> BCD Travel
> Orlando, Florida, U.S.
> Phone: (407) 514-3285, Ext. 7
> Email: heather.smith@bcdtravel.com

(This company handles the travel arrangements for Campus Crusade for Christ and for Saddleback Valley Community Church)

For hotel bookings and transportation within Kenya:

> Stonic Koipah
> Entiak Maasai Travel Ltd
> P.O Box 3936-00200
> Nairobi, KENYA
> Email: koipah@yahoo.com

Anyone interested in joining a group led by Pastor Steve Rutenbar can get information by email: kenya@saddleback.net

9   **If I visit her, what should I take with me for Sister Freda?**
Contact Sister Freda to learn her current needs. Single bed sheets are in constant demand. When they tear, they are made into crib sheets or bandages. Baby clothing and

blankets are a special blessing. Also needed are adult and children's vitamins, but check expiration dates — people in Kenya do not profit from nor appreciate outdated medicines any more than we do in the U.S., and Kenya has strict standards about this. If in doubt about what to bring, ask her and she will tell you her most current need.

Sr. Freda's Medical Center
P. O. Box 696
Kitale 30200
Kenya (East Africa)

10 **Can we adopt any of these children?** Kenya is one of the strictest countries in Africa on the issue of adoption. You would have to go through an American agency that would work with a Kenyan attorney and Kenyan Welfare Department officer. You must reside in Kenya for three months, and the whole process takes about three years. In most cases it is better to give money for the care of the children in Kenya. Sister Freda can always find a qualified "mother" who is willing to care for a needy child because she knows the local women well. This approach helps in two ways:
    a. The child is well cared for in his own culture
    b. The mother is provided with income to feed her own children as well
    c. Cost: $30 a month

Endnotes

FOREWORD

[1] 300,000 in refugee camps and perhaps another 200,000 housed with friends and relatives.

[2] Edwin Okong'o, "Kenya: Playing the Tribe Card," http://www.pbs.org/frontlineworld/blog/2008/01kenyaplayingt.html

[3] "Kenya: Rights Activist Pushes for UN Action," Interview of Maina Kiai with Katy Gabel, Brian Kennedy and intern Katie Wyly of AllAfrica's Washington office, allafrica.com, http://allafrica.com/stories/200802120297.html, February 12, 2008.

[4] Emily Wax, Washington Post Foreign Service, September 18, 2005, A01.

[5] Edwin Okong'o, Ibid.

[6] Maina Kiai, Ibid.

[7] http://ritch-african.blogspot.com/2006/08/tribalism-kenyas-oldest-living.html, August 23, 2006.

[8] Maina Kiai, Ibid.

Chapter 2
BORN TO CARE

[1] A type of corn that is Africa's primary source of food. http://www.theglobalist.com/StoryId.aspx?StoryId=4887

[2] The drought in East Africa in recent years has caused shortage of food and loss of cattle in such numbers that some tribesmen are trading their daughters in marriage at ages as young as eight and nine in exchange for a few cows, some blankets and cash or access to grazing land.

Edmund Sanders, "In Bad Times, Girls Become Prime Financial Assets," Los Angeles Times, March 19, 2006, A10.

Chapter 3
LIFE-SAVING HOSPITAL CARE

[1] *Ugali* is a staple starch component of many African meals. It is generally made from maize flour and water and varies in consistency from porridge to a dough-like substance. *Ugali* is inexpensive to make and the flour can last for considerable time. Also, the crops that produce the corn flour grow reliably in poor seasons. For these reasons, *ugali* is an important part of the diet of millions of Africans.

Chapter 4
THE POWER OF PRAYER

[1] Randall D. Roth, *Prayer Powerpoints* (Wheaton, IL: Victor Books, 1995), 58.

Chapter 5
PROMPTED BY COMPASSION

[1] From a report by Dr. Trey Wilson, D.D.S. aired May 29, 2007 on CNN's "Heroes" feature. Taken from CNN "Heroes" feature 5-29-07. http://www.cnn.com/video/player/player.html?url=/video/specials/2007/05/29/heroes.wilson.call.to.action.cnn

Chapter 6
IN CRISIS

[1] From a letter to Megan Affleck, January 29, 2008.
[2] From an email to Chuck and Sue Wells, ICM Ministries, quoted in their email newsletter, Vol. 2, Issue 2, dated February 2008.
[3] http://ohioline.osu.edu/hyg-fact/2000/2100.html; http://insects.tamu.edu/extension/bulletins/L-1223.html

Chapter 7
BRINGING HOPE TO WOMEN AND CHILDREN
[1] From "World Fact Book.doc – Kenya," last updated January 20, 2006.
https://www.cia.gov/cia/publications/factbook/geos/ke.html#top
[2] "FGM in Kenya: Outlawed, Not Eradicated," Ochieng' Ogodo,
WeNews correspondent, February 8, 2005.
http://www.womensenews.org/article.cfm/dyn/aid/2177
[3] Esther and Lucy are being supported through Fruited Plains, Inc.,
headed by Mike and Michele Robison. See www.fruitedplains.org
[4] "Policy on orphans ready, says Awori," by Mike Mwaniki,
published 1/30/07
http://www.nationmedia.com/dailynation/
nmgcontententry.asp?categoryid=1&newsid=90641

Chapter 8
IN TIMES OF DISCOURAGEMENT
[1] David Stevens, M.D., *Jesus, M.D.* (Grand Rapids, MI: Zondervan,
2001), 75.

Chapter 9
THE BIG FOUR
[1] Brucellosis is a serious bacterial disease that causes fever, joint pain and
fatigue. Although the bacteria can spread through the air or through
direct contact with infected animals, most people get brucellosis from
unpasteurized dairy products. Brucellosis can usually be treated
successfully with antibiotics, but the regimen is lengthy and relapses are
common, even after treatment. There is no vaccine for brucellosis in
humans. Sister Freda says it's usually contracted from animals,
unpasteurized milk and undercooked meat, but it can also be
transmitted in breast milk. From www.mayoclinic.com

[2] "Wife Inheritance Spurs AIDS Rise in Kenya," Stephen Buckley, Washington Post Foreign Service, November 8, 1997. http://www.washingtonpost.com/wp-rv/inatl/longterm/africanlssives/kenyha/kenya_aids.htm#TOP

[3] WHO Assessment of the Epidemiological Situation http://web.worldbank.org/WBSITE/EXTERNAL/COUNTRIES/AFRICAEXT/EXTAFRHEANUTPOP/EXTAFRREGTOPHIVAIDS/0,,contentMDK:20435845~pagePK:34004173~piPK:34003707~theSitePK:717148,00.html

[4] http://www.dfid.gov.uk/news/files/pressreleases/bednets-info.asp

[5] http://www.psi.org/where_we_work/kenya.html . Page last updated: 03/09/2007.

[6] http://www.uyaphi.com/kenya/malaria.htm, 2005

[7] www.hinduonnet.com/2006/01/04/stories/2006010409841100.htm-21k-

[8] www.thestatesmanonline.com/pages/news_detail.php?section=1&newsid=75 - 34k

[9] Go to coffeeinfo@verizon.net to purchase delicious Kenyan coffee. The proceeds will go to help the work of Sister Freda.

[10] http://www.kenyaspace.com/churchesinkenya.htm

Chapter 14
THE FACILITATOR

[1] http://thinkexist.com/quotation/there-is-no-limit-to-what-can-be-accomplished-if/406865.html

[2] The film was later nominated for Best Documentary of the Year award at Chapman.

[3] The boys have the same birth mother, but different fathers, and the birth mother doesn't know who the fathers are. She was 21 when the boys were adopted, so she was probably pregnant with Derek at age 14 and gave birth at age 15.

Chapter 16
"TELL THEM TO COME"
[1] John Piper, *Desiring God* (Portland, OR: Multnomah Press, 1986), 104.

Chapter 17
BUILDING A BRIDGE
[1] David Stevens, M.D. with Gregg Lewis, *Jesus, M.D.* (Grand Rapids, MI: Zondervan, 2001), 79.
[2] As quoted by Janet Parshall on February 17, 2007 at the opening session of National Religious Broadcasters Convention.
[3] Ravi Zacharias with R.S.B. Sawyer, *Walking From East to West* (Grand Rapids, MI: Zondervan, 2006), 223.

WHAT KENYANS SAY
ABOUT SISTER FREDA

"Sister Freda is a great woman for us. She has a heart for our Kenyan poor, for our mothers and children who suffer. She gathered the courage to move to Birunda Village to found a hospital where those who cannot afford medical care can come for help. As a clinician, I have watched what is happening. When I saw how Sister Freda charges only what they are able to pay, I was so impressed and encouraged. She puts their lives ahead of anything else. Seeing her intentions and motives, I can truly say that she deserves support."

> **Dr. James Akudian**
> *Clinical Officer, Kitale District Hospital,*
> *and top medical official for the Pokot Tribe.*

"We pay a small amount on a monthly basis for her to treat our staff and kids, which means their care comes at a big discount. She handles our emergencies and needs for hospital care. Some of the local hospitals will not admit street kids — 'We don't want them — they're too dirty.' Sister Freda will always take them in."

> **Geoffrey Okumu**
> *Director of Oasis of Hope School and Ministry to more*
> *than 100 street kids of Matisi in Kitale, Kenya.*

"At other hospitals patients have to deposit 20,000 Kenyan schillings (nearly $300) before being admitted, but Sister Freda admits people regardless of their ability to pay. I have the utmost admiration for Sister Freda, and she will always be my example to follow."

> **Dr. Daniel Kibet Tanui**
>
> *Director of Kaplamai Health Center, a District (government) Hospital in Trans-Nzoia, where Kitale is located. Founder of Mustard Seed International, which began with a small clinic for treating those who can afford to pay little or nothing, after the pattern of Sister Freda, his model and mentor. Since 2005, Dr. Tanui has volunteered with Sister Freda, doing ward rounds and surgery. He also follows in her footsteps by paying for the costs of sending patients to Nairobi for advanced treatment.*

"When I met Sister Freda In 1999, I immediately sensed her heart for working with destitute people. She had compassion for street kids. When she learned that Oasis of Hope was open, up and running, she felt a heart-tug and offered to help the kids with their medical needs. Sister Freda also treats our church members, who pay only a minimum amount for care — or nothing, if they cannot afford to pay."

> **Pastor Moses Zewedi**
>
> *Lives Changing Ministries, Kitale, Kenya.*

". . . a wonderful woman full of compassion."

> **Agnes Makhanu**
>
> *Pharmacist.*

"Freda is a minister of touching people for God with His love. She is unique. She believes not only in her profession but also that God truly heals today. God is in her ministering to people. People she has treated heal very fast — beyond normal healing. She points people to God, very aware that, as Jesus said, 'Apart from me, you can do nothing' (John 15:5). God uses her to reveal Himself to people. She is an agent of change in our society."

Rev. Ezekiel Kisaka
Pastor of Emmanuel Worship Center,
Kitale, Kenya.

"I was attended by Sr. Freda when three of my four children were born, and the fourth, who was born in Mombasa, has been treated at Sister Freda's hospital—by choice. While she was still on staff at Mt. Elgon Hospital, I asked for her to attend me because Sister Freda is always smiling, always checking on her patients beyond her duty and beyond her professional calling as a nurse. When she established her hospital, I wanted to go where she was. In her hospital I felt I was not in a hospital but at home. It is so *clean* and the food is like homemade food, not hospital food. It's not a beautiful, expensive building that counts but the person who makes the difference. If you asked my friends, they'd say they want Sister Freda. In town they call her 'the Great Nurse.' "

Dr. Dorothy Masinde
Sociologist, School of Agriculture of Iowa State
University, and Program Coordinator for the
Center for Sustainable Rural Livelihood in Uganda;
long-time friend of Freda's.

"Sister Freda assisted in the birth of all eight of us children and treated our entire family for all this time. What I appreciate about Sister Freda is that she is so active in talking to her patients; she receives them so warmly, she listens with undivided attention and really cares so much. Her clinic is well-known for its cleanliness and low rates she charges, treating both rich and poor. She is loving and knows how to deal with everybody. And the quality of her care? The best!"

> ⋇ **Ann**
>
> *Resident of Kitale, Kenya.*

"Talk to any woman in Kitale — she knows of Sister Freda. When she resigned from her position at Mt. Elgon Hospital as Hospital Matron (hospital administrator, in charge of all departments), it was one of three major hospitals in this region of Africa — Kenyatta General Hospital in Nairobi and one in Uganda being the other two — the people of Kitale protested. Mt. Elgon Hospital is a facility for those who can pay 300 Kenyan schillings ($45) a day. Sister Freda's Hospital is the poor man's hospital, planned that way by Sister Freda. She is a wonderful person. She has a mind for the poor.

Four of my five children were delivered by her — and the fifth would have been but arrived before we could get to her hospital. Ten years ago I was in a terrible traffic accident caused by a drunk driver. I was flown to Nairobi for care and was in a coma for twenty-one days. I had many surgeries. After two months, I was brought back home. Sister Freda would visit me two or three times a week. She also sent a therapist to my home to help me. I am extremely grateful to her."

> ⋇ **Shem S. K. Amai**
>
> *Chief of Kilomet area, government official who is responsible for 50,000 people in the Kitale area, of whom he knows 45% personally. He serves as the go-between for them with the President of Kenya.*